A SOLUTION OF STRESS WITH NUTRIENTS

Proper nutrition for stress and diseases of the nervous system

Jack Bracknell

Contents

Abstract

This book is devoted to the recently popular topic proper nutrition for stress and diseases of the nervous system. AT it also provides recommendations of traditional medicine that will help not only improve the patient's condition, but in some cases even completely get rid of nervous disorders and reduce the manifestation of stressful situations on the body to a minimum.

Introduction

In today's world, stress is becoming more and more dangerous for every person. They negatively affect the physical and emotional state of a person, his ability to make the right decision at the right time. Often, systematic stress causes the development of such diseases of the nervous system, such as migraine, atherosclerosis, osteochondritis, etc. And here it is very important to notice the connection in time and start treatment correctly.

With stress and many diseases of the nervous system, significant relief, as has been noted, is provided by a change in diet. Food rich in all the necessary substances: fats, proteins, carbohydrates, trace elements, fiber and vitamins, can significantly improve the patient's condition. So, the doctor found out that patients suffering from a disease resembling schizophrenia in symptoms quickly felt significant relief if they were given foods rich in B vitamins.

In addition to a balanced diet or even a diet, herbal decoctions, bee products, etc. may be required. However, as a rule, there is always a result, even if the disease is complex and diet alone is not enough. And in diseases such as, for example, atherosclerosis, diet, on the contrary, plays a major role in the treatment.

The book discusses stress in detail: its causes, symptoms of leakage, ways to get rid of it by changing the diet. The following describes diseases of the nervous system and how to treat them with a balanced diet, decoctions and traditional medicine. However, following the recommendations given in this book, we must not forget that in no case should you try to self-medicate. If you suspect a particular disease, it is best to consult a doctor who will prescribe the appropriate treatment. And as an additional remedy, you can use the recommendations below.

CHAPTER 1 STRESS

Michel de Montaigne (1533–1592), a French philosopher and writer, once said: “Health is a treasure, and, moreover, the only one for which it is really worth not only not sparing time, effort, labor and all kinds of benefits, but also sacrificing for the sake of him a particle of life itself, since life without it becomes unbearable and humiliating.

In the modern world, a person lives under the yoke of a severe lack of time and energy. An adult spends most of his life at work, a child in kindergarten, a teenager in school, and young people in secondary or higher educational institutions. At the same time, about a third of personal time is spent on sleep and eating. Of course, in such conditions, the time that you can devote to yourself, friends and relatives is very limited, and even more so it is not enough for long and often expensive procedures to maintain your health at the proper level.

As a rule, an ordinary average person seeks help from doctors only when the body begins to directly signal existing problems through pain or any other symptoms. Unfortunately, in this case, a simple medical intervention is often no longer enough to restore the previous performance. And then doctors and surgeons get to work. Alas, few people take the trouble to think that by paying a little more attention to your body, you can reduce the risk of this kind of ailment.

The human body is a surprisingly complex and multifunctional system with a huge number of processes occurring inside it, ranging from simple physical to complex energy. Mentioning this in his works, I. P. Pavlov, a well-known Russian researcher, wrote: "The human body is a highly self-regulating system that directs, maintains, restores and even improves itself."

Indeed, a sufficiently fragile human body has an amazing ability to maintain the balance of all processes in itself, and this ensures its efficiency. However, despite the apparent strength of this complex organic system, it should not be abandoned to its fate. It is necessary to create and carefully maintain a system of conditions that will help the body to communicate with both the external and internal world. We should also not forget that it is necessary to take carc of your body systematically, and not from time to time, when the need arises.

Surprisingly, if in the past, especially in the Middle Ages, the main various infectious diseases, such as plague and cholera, posed a threat to human health, now the list of the most common and dangerous diseases has been replenished with stress. Indeed, according to the American Academy of Family Physicians, more than 70% of people who seek medical help in countries with a developed industry, economy and social institution have suffered from stress in one way or another.

It should be clarified that stress is a somewhat conditional and individual concept. In other words, for each person it is subjective, manifests itself in different situations with different symptoms and intensity. For one, stress may be caused by a divorce or the death of a loved one, for another, a car ride or too much noise. In both cases, stress can be accompanied by similar symptoms and equally adversely affect health.

Modern people, especially those living within the boundaries of a large and busy city, are faced with situations that can cause stress almost every hour. Commenting on this situation in his recent speech during a tour of the United States, the head of the English National Institute of Mental Health said: “The whole world is under stress. It is one of the fastest growing diseases in the world."

Stress is the cause of many interpersonal conflicts. And how a person copes with it depends on his well-being and how others will treat him. Studies have shown that in such an economically developed country as the united States, a huge number of people do not show up for their jobs due to stress. The material costs of their treatment and the overall decline in labor productivity in monetary terms annually amount to more than 500 million dollars. According to forecasts, by 2010 this figure will increase to 88 billion dollars. Scientists are sounding the alarm, trying to draw people's attention to this problem. So what is stress and how can it be treated?

Physiology of Stress

Stress is a strong nervous tension caused by the action of some strong stimulus. Perhaps, a stressful state can be called a response protective reaction of the human body to some influence from both the person's own mind and the environment.

To put it simply, stress is a life phenomenon. It invades in the early morning along with the sunbeams or the insistent ringing of the alarm clock. Throughout the day, human nerves are subjected to a serious test of strength. A conflict at work, a quarrel with a loved one, a trip on public transport, a long queue, the lack of desired attention from others - all this causes tension in the nervous system, and therefore can cause stress. Even at night, a person does not know peace, poor sleep can not only spoil the mood, but also lead to a serious imbalance in the internal balance of the body.

Experts studying the work of the nervous system have come to the conclusion that people cannot live without stress. If there is no external irritant, a person immediately invents one for himself. Complexes, conjectures and suspicions, usually unjustified, quickly bring the nervous system into a state of readiness to repel an imaginary threat. However, the absence of visible danger and the unwillingness of the mind to part with its obsession disorient the body and again provoke stress.

The concept of "stress" entered the medical terminology relatively recently. The well-known Canadian biologist G. Selye first used this word in 1936. The term itself has English roots and is translated into Russian as “tension”. A little later, the scientist identified 3 stages of stress and submitted his theory to the consideration of colleagues.

According to G. Selva, stress has a three-phase development. At the first stage, which he called the “anxiety stage”, the body, having felt anxiety, begins to mobilize all its reserves to resist it. At the second stage, the stage of resistance, comprehension of the situation and adaptation to new conditions begin. In the third stage, which Salve called “stage of exhaustion" the body, which has been in tension for a long time, begins to feel severe fatigue, often accompanied by depression.

Stress can be both beneficial and harmful. In a stressful state, a person mobilizes internal reserves in order to adapt to new conditions - this is what allows him to adapt and survive in any, the most unfavorable conditions. On the other hand, strong and prolonged nervous tension can lead to a rapid loss of body capacity and its destruction. Perhaps in this case it is possible to draw an analogy with the physical efforts: optimally selected load helps to develop muscles, and excessive leads to exhaustion of the body.

When a person feels stress, the body begins to produce epinephrine and norepinephrine. The first of these doctors often call the stress hormone. Getting into the blood, it causes significant changes in the work of the human body: the blood glucose content increases, the heart begins to beat faster, blood pressure rises rapidly. At the peak of these changes, the strength and dexterity of a person increase, the brain begins to work more intensively in order to identify the cause of irritation as quickly as possible and get rid of it.

From all this we can conclude that a short light stress in itself is not dangerous. Problems appear at the moment when one stressful situation is superimposed on another, a third one joins them, etc. Unfortunately, the recovery capabilities of the human body are not as great as we would like, therefore, in order to recover from the consequences of even one mild stress, the body may take more than one day.

Frequent stress over time leads to the appearance of nervous disorders of varying severity. In advanced cases, atherosclerosis, angina pectoris, duodenal ulcers, ischemia, hypertension, immunodeficiency, and stomach ulcers may develop. The risk of heart attacks and strokes increases.

The following are symptoms of severe stress that you should immediately contact a specialist for help:

– sweaty palms;

– headpain;

– nervous tic;

– itching;

– shiver;

– constant anxiety;

– dizziness;

– loss of consciousness;

– bleeding fromnose

– throat bleeding orrectum;

– frequentpulse;

– too rare or vice versa frequent breathing;

– chronic headache;

– constant discomfort in the area neck and back;

– rash;

– insomnia;

– drowsiness;

– irritability;

– unreasonable aggressiveness.

The famous doctor A. Roche once said: "The basic rule is this: you should see a doctor if you have not had such symptoms before and they have no obvious cause, especially if they impair the quality of life."

However, stress does not always

lead to the development of dangerous and chronic diseases. At present, when a stressful situation is the norm of life, many people develop many ailments that, at first glance, have nothing to do with psychological discomfort and stress. For example, young people suffer from acne and obesity, men from hair loss, women from infertility. At the same time, victims often do not understand what caused their misfortune, but the answer is simple.

Indeed, severe stress often causes severe hair loss. During this period of life, when a person is constantly experiencing shocks, not necessarily unpleasant, such as a wedding, the birth of a child, or a move, the amount of hair that has fallen out can increase. However, don't blame it on stress alone. Hair falls out constantly. No matter how good a person's health is, he loses more than 70 hairs every day. And the intake of certain medications, hormonal and age-related changes can also provoke a stronger loss.

Stress negatively affects the condition of the skin. Experts have confirmed that strong nervous shocks often cause acne formations. This situation is especially typical for people who have crossed the 20-year milestone.

Although teenagers are more likely than adults to suffer from acne, the cause of their ailments, as a rule, is the usual hormonal changes. However, unusually high excitability people aged 12 to 18 provokes stress in them 3 times more often than in adults, and this cannot be ignored.

American scientists confirmed the opinion of Russian experts that severe stress may well cause infertility. The mechanism of this phenomenon is not entirely clear, especially since some scientists believe in the existence of a double link between cause and effect. That is, just as stress can cause infertility, infertility often puts a person in a stressful state.

Stress can provoke rapid weight gain and, as a result, the development of obesity. The fact is that very often people, wanting to suppress unpleasant emotions or relieve nervous tension, begin to eat a lot. Tears are a great way to relieve stress, however, by reducing nervous tension in this way, a person also begins to feel severe hunger.

Unfortunately, a person is far from always able to determine whether he has stress or not. Since stress is a protective reaction of the body, its main function is to provide a person with such conditions that will help him survive in the most dangerous and unusual situations when quick action is required, and not long reflections. Moreover, the weaker the stress, the better the person will feel it, and accordingly, with very strong stress, the symptoms, as a rule, appear only after the elimination of the irritant and the reduction of nervous tension.

Susceptibility to stress can be both

genetic and acquired. The most vulnerable in this regard, scientists consider people with a strong-willed character, leading an active lifestyle, such as actors, directors of large enterprises, politicians and TV presenters. In an attempt to achieve their goal, they exhaust their body, not giving it time to rest and recuperate. Overload causes stress, and then increasing fatigue.

Trying to relieve stress, but not wanting to give yourself a rest, a person can resort to various stimulants, such as alcohol, tobacco, coffee and drugs.

Tobacco products, which are in such high demand in our time, are considered by many to be a panacea for all ills. But is it? Indeed, smoking a cigarette can reduce nervous tension for a while, but this helps to distract from the problem only for a short time, and does not solve it and does not relieve stress. The same is true with drugs. Their action passes, and the problems and caused they stress remain.

As for caffeine, it is absolutely not suitable for stress relief. The fact is that when it enters the body, this substance begins to stimulate it, prompting it to produce more and more adrenaline, the stress hormone. Thus, a person who wants to reduce tension and drinks a little coffee for this purpose will achieve exactly the opposite result.

But alcohol can really have a relaxing effect, of course, if it is consumed at the right time and in small quantities. However, alcohol is still not the ideal remedy for all problems. A slight intoxication can be very useful, but should not be relied upon. It is best to rely on other means to solve your problems.

Stress is a very interesting human reaction. Its uniqueness lies in the fact that its causes are usually psychological. Moreover, each of these reasons represents two equivalent, closely intertwined factors: the first is the problem that provoked stress, the second is the person's reaction to the current situation. The fact is that in most cases stress is caused not by the problem itself as such, but by the person's attitude towards it, his thoughts and emotions.

T. H. Holmes, a well-known psychiatrist, developed an unusual scale to determine the level of stress in the life of an average person, based on which one can find out with what force certain events act on the body. It lists various events that a person may experience in life, and provides stress levels calculated on a 100-point scale.

1. Death of a spouse - 100.

2. Divorce - 73.

3. Separation from spouse - 65.

4. Serving a prison sentence - 63.

5. Death of a close family member - 63.

6. Personal bodily injury or illness - 53.

7. Marriage (marriage) - 50.

8. Dismissal from work - 47.

9. Settlement of disputes in the marital life - 45.

10. Retirement (retirement) - 45.

11. State change health of a family member - 44.

12. Pregnancy - 40.

13. sexual problems- 39.

14. Replenishmentin the family - 39.

15. Entryin business - 39.

16. Change in financial position - 38.

17. Death of a close friend - 37.

18. Change of occupation (activity) - 36.

19. Changing the frequency of disputes with a spouse- 35.

20. Mortgage for an amount exceeding10 thousand dollars - 31.

21. Deprivation of the debtor of the right to redeem the property pledged by him or the loan (loan) - 30.

22. Changing the degree of responsibility at work– 29.

23. Son or daughter leaves home - 29.

24. Problem with relativeswife (husband) - 29.

25. Outstanding Individual Achievement - 28.

26. wife startsor stops working - 26.

27. Start or end of study - 26.

28. Change in living conditions- 25.

29. revisionpersonal habits - 24.

30. Boss problem - 23.

31. Changing the mode and working conditions - 20.

32. Change of residence - 20.

33. Change of school - 20.

34. Changing the method of conducting leisure - 19.

35. Changes related to church activities - 19.

36. Changing social activities - 17.

37. Mortgage or loan in the amount of less than 10 thousand dollars - 17.

38. Changes in sleep mode - 16.

39. Change in the number of joint family gatherings - 15.

40. Changediet - 15.

41. Vacation (holidays) - 13.

42. Christmas - 12.

43. Minor violationslaw - 11.

Personality types and their reactions to stress

The main problem of people is a partial or complete unwillingness to control their emotions. Holding back, they are guided rather by the requirements of etiquette and the fear of attracting the attention of law enforcement agencies. But the correct and correct management of emotions is not only following the rules, but also undoubted health benefits.

Emotional control helps to rationally distribute one's strength, manage behavior and avoid severe stress. Unfortunately, only a very small number of people know how to do this, and interpersonal relationships, and, consequently, the neutralization of stressful situations, depend on the ability to keep their feelings under control.

Since it is the attitude of a person to a situation that determines whether a stimulus will cause stress or not, one should take a closer look at the various personal characteristics of certain types of people who react to a stressful situation in different ways, depending on their internal beliefs.

Relatively recently, specialists dealing with this problem have identified six such types:

– cheerful;

– phlegmatic;

– aggressive;

– pedantic;

– passive;

excitable.Cheerfulpersonality type

This type includes energetic and strong people living an active life. They love to communicate, impulsive and friendly.

These can be politicians, artists, actors, traveling salesmen, entertainers, fashion designers and writers.

Cheerful people get along well with others, trying not to go into conflict, but they are able to kick back. Stress for them often becomes not any life situation, but inaction, causing boredom.

Phlegmatic personality type

This type includes calm, dreamy people. They are inactive, prefer to spend time passively contemplating some non-binding image, such as an aquarium fish, clouds, stars, trees, paintings, etc.

Phlegmatic people often remember their past, do not like change and almost do not give in to stress. They carefully control their lives, trying to pay equal attention to both work and family. This behavioral stereotype is typical of American housewives, zookeepers, and scientists.

Strangers can provoke a stressful situation, imposing some unusual norms of behavior on phlegmatic, or pushing those to unpleasant actions. Any disruption to a normal lifestyle can lead to stress and ultimately depression.

Aggressive personality type

The aggressive personality type refers to people who have a strong need for personal growth and the success of everything conceived. These include social workers, managers, and directors of small but growing businesses, athletes, entertainers and actors.

They show great physical and mental activity, energetic and domineering. All their energy is spent on achieving the goal, to which they go, not paying attention to the opinions of the people around them.

Stress in such individuals can be caused by too hard work and inability to properly manage their forces, conflicts in the family and personal complexes. As a rule, people who get into a stressful situation are disturbed by sleep, problems with digestion, heart and blood pressure appear. Often, under the pressure of circumstances, they begin to use alcohol, tobacco and drugs.

Pedantic personality type

This type of people primarily includes pedantic, petty, conservative, meticulous and stubborn personalities. Above all, they put stability and obligations, trust only recognized authorities, are very law-abiding, strictly adhere to etiquette and traditions.

Pedantic people are very vulnerable to stress, and many factors can cause it, such as a sudden change in environment or other people. Any violation of the usual daily routine or plans can lead to stress, which a pedantic person endures very hard.

Passive personality type

This type includes soft, flexible people who are not able to show character, defending their rights. They avoid conflicts by all means, even to the detriment of themselves, please more strong-willed people and experience internal discomfort from communicating with another person.

Fear of a possible confrontation and the idea that you need to make some kind of decision, and then implement it, can lead a passive type person into a state of stress, then depression, then possible hysteria, culminating in an outbreak of suicidal aspirations.

Excitable personality type

People of this type weakly resist stress. The excitability of the nervous system leads to the fact that even taking a bath can turn into a serious test for an excitable person. Especially if it is accompanied by some not the most pleasant thoughts.

Low self-esteem, suspiciousness and an abundance of various complexes serve as constant sources of irritation for excitable people. It can be exacerbated by dramatic changes in lifestyle or any difficult work for which you have to bear responsibility.

Stress test and personality type

This test is recommended to pass to determine your vulnerability to domestic stress. To do this, it is necessary to fill in the table every day in the evening for a week, filling in those columns that correspond to a positive answer to the question. Determination of susceptibility to stress type of personality each shaded column corresponds to one point. After filling the table points are summed up.

If the number of points does not exceed 20, there is no cause for alarm. Usually this situation is typical for people with an aggressive and cheerful type of character.

People who scored from 21 to 40 points, as a rule, correspond to the phlegmatic personality type. This situation is not very dangerous. A bit of self-control and an effort to eliminate the factors that cause anxiety will probably lead to a stabilization of the situation.

People who score from 41 to 60 points are at great risk to their health. In this case, drastic measures are needed to eliminate the discomfort. This situation is typical for the pedantic and passive type of personality, which are especially vulnerable to stress.

Only a few people score more than 60 points, these are mostly excitable individuals who are unable or unwilling to control their emotions. This situation is very alarming and requires the immediate help of a specialist.

Types of stress

Scientists divide stress into several main varieties: psychological (emotional), physiological (informational), long-term (chronic), short-term (acute), positive and negative.

Psychological stress acts on the nervous system with great force, although it does not have external clearly expressed negative consequences. As a rule, it is caused by problems in personal and family life, such as the death or illness of a loved one, marriage, divorce or the birth of a child.

Physiological stress is a consequence of the impact on the human body of such negative factors as heat, cold, pain, pleasure, thirst, hunger, etc.

Long-term and short-term stress affect the state of the body in different ways. The most difficult of them is the first one.

Characteristic features of short-term stress are the unexpectedness and speed with which it occurs. If the stress is very strong, the person may go into a state of shock. As a rule, this occurs when situations arise that do not correspond to a person's life experience, such as natural disasters or major catastrophes, such as war or revolution, as well as inflation.

A state of shock can quickly turn into chronic long-term stress, when, even after a long time after the experience, memories of the experienced return, disturbing the emotional balance of a person.

Information stress appears as a result of a strong information overstrain. If a person who is forced to make many responsible decisions ceases to optimally distribute his forces or simply does not have time to do this, a stressful situation arises. Its frequent victims, as a rule, are control operators of some mechanized systems, car drivers, directors of large enterprises, law enforcement officers, programmers, students, etc.

Some types of stress, the most typical, are discussed below. Stress caused by an inferiority complex the term "inferiority complex" was coined by Alfred Adler, a well-known psychiatrist from Germany. He believed that this complex is both negative and positive.

Of course, most people have to deal with the negative impact of the inferiority complex on the psyche and body one way or another. A person who feels inferior is almost constantly in a state of nervous excitement, turning either into depression or into a stage of aggressive activity. The stronger the complex, the more unpredictably the person behaves.

The reason for the emergence of an inferiority complex can be any factor somehow connected with a person's life, but first of all, one that concerns his personal qualities, for example, appearance, intelligence, character, taste, behavior, etc. Often the complex has a far-fetched meaning when man himself invents it, guided by characteristics of a fictitious ideal or the statements of others. In order to determine if a person has a complex inferiority, experienced psychologists offer him to answer on the a few questions, for example:

1. Do you think yourself beautiful?

2. Do you consider yourself smart?

3. Are you satisfied with your height?

4. Do you like your hair color?

5. How often do you change sexual partners?

6. Do you like to communicate with people?

7. Do you love yourself?

If a person gives a positive or indefinite answer to most of these questions, his inferiority complex is poorly developed, if negative, it is worth paying attention to.

Paradoxically, there are no people in the world who have no complexes at all. Even if a person does not realize this, there is still a so-called irritant in his subconscious, which is not always possible to notice, but it is he who, getting into a favorable environment, often provokes a stressful situation. For example, a person who subconsciously considers himself clumsy, having come to the company of athletes, begins to feel even more awkward, which immediately causes a stress reaction.

However, Alfred Adler considered the inferiority complex to be very useful in the sense that it forces a person to improve himself, to look for ways to solve existing problems.

A striking example of this, the

psychologist believed, was Napoleon Bonaparte, who was distinguished by his small stature, but compensated for this shortcoming with his activity, charm and determination.

The famous military figure became famous for his victories, accomplished not only on the battlefield, but also on the love front. He was considered not only an outstanding commander and politician, but also a wonderful lover. At the same time, Napoleon's short stature was perceived not as a disadvantage, but as an undoubted advantage, emphasizing his outstanding mind.

Adler believed that it was Napoleon's inferiority complex that brought this Frenchman to fame and opened his way to the throne. Currently, many representatives of the stronger sex are complex because of their small stature, dense physique or non-athletic figure, not even suspecting that it is men of small stature who are considered excellent lovers. The fact is that, unlike tall athletic rivals, it is more difficult for short men to attract the attention of a beautiful woman, and therefore they try to overcome this difficulty by developing talents that will help compensate for the lack of small stature, such as eloquence, intelligence, etc.

A person is imperfect, and during his life he often finds himself in situations where he begins to realize his imperfection, but still such a feeling of inferiority cannot be called a complex.

An inferiority complex is only an awareness of one's inferiority experienced throughout life. But people are different, and what for one is a serious disadvantage, in the eyes of another may look like an undoubted advantage. Therefore, having an inferiority complex, one must treat him like an old picky friend - compromise with him and avoid conflicts that can cause stress.

Ignoring your complex or pretending that it does not exist is not a way out. In the eyes of an attentive observer, it will look as if a person were walking down the street, covering a large tear in his clothes with his hand, but as soon as you remove your palm, the "complex" is clearly visible.

Do not forget that the inferiority complexes that so often poison life are not a real confirmation of a person's inferiority, but rather an awareness of it, which often does not correspond to the truth at all.

An inferiority complex can bring any person to severe stress, depression, exhaustion and, ultimately, suicide. With such a complex it is necessary to fight, leaving him no chance of survival. Experts are sure that it is stress caused by an inferiority complex that has the most devastating effect on a person's life. It is the longest and difficult to overcome, because it is supported by the subconscious of a person.

Stress caused by romantic experiences

The concept of "love" is very voluminous, but completely subjective. And at the same time, speaking about his love, a person implies the existence of positive emotions directed at some creature. At all times it was believed that love gives only positive emotions, but this is not so. Jealousy, the pain of the rejected, the joy of meeting and even a banal touch - all this carries a huge emotional charge, and therefore leads to the appearance of stress loads. Psychologists often say that in terms of stress, the death of a loved one is equivalent to the birth of a child or two weddings. The difference between negative and positive emotions in this regard does not matter, since stress is just the sum of the physiological and psychological reactions of the human body. Thus, the strength of stress that arose in response to negative and positive events is approximately the same.

It often happens that a person's romantic feelings do not resonate with another, especially in the first stage of their relationship. Surprisingly, in this situation, both parties are equally stressed. Many people believe that only the person who confesses his love suffers from unrequited feelings, and the one who confessed it does not. In fact, the situation is more complicated.

The one who loves, of course, is unhappy that he is not reciprocated. The range of various emotions, from which the lover either cries or ascends to the pinnacle of bliss, is nothing in front of the psychological state of the one to whom these feelings are directed.

The object of admiration of the lover experiences even more stress than the lover himself. There is a sense of guilt, and anxiety, and pity, and awkwardness. Often there are situations when a man who has gone on a one-time and completely random sexual contact, after its completion, comes to complete despair, because he thinks that he is obliged to somehow continue the relationship that has arisen. A similar situation develops in the event that a woman succumbs to sexual pressure from a partner, not daring to refuse him because of fear of the consequences.

In both cases, the relationship between random partners will not lead to a positive result. The stress experienced by both parties can become long-term and ultimately lead to tragedy. To avoid such an ending, it is necessary first of all to explain to a loved one that he can make his choice, and is not at all obliged to reciprocate.

It should not be forgotten that if a person who is loved is disturbed, then in some way he will try to distance himself from the factor that causes inconvenience and stress. He will start to avoid his admirer or move to more aggressive actions.

The understanding that the lover will not put pressure on him or somehow force him to respond will allow him to maintain calm and understanding in the relationship. Of course, this will not mean that the lover has abandoned his feelings or intentions, it's just that in the end the object of these claims will no longer feel anxiety, his stress level will decrease, and the person will be able to objectively evaluate his fan, so that then it's possible to still reciprocate his the senses.

As regards so-called unhappy love, when, despite all the efforts of a lover, the object of his admiration refuses to reciprocate, it can be dangerous not only for the emotional state of a person, but also for his health. The English scientist Frank Tallies found that severe stress caused by emotional outbursts often leads to an outbreak of very dangerous hormones. Their release is accompanied by symptoms similar to those that appear in a person with a heart attack.

Thus, unrequited love and the emotions it evokes contribute to long-term stress. It is very dangerous for human life, and the accompanying nervous and emotional excitement contribute to the development of many diseases. In some cases, a desperate person, unable to get rid of stress, decides to commit suicide.

Unrequited love has been studied by doctors for many years as a curious and rather dangerous disease. Approximately 200 years ago, in most medical reference books there was a description of the so-called love disease, which was considered intractable and the most common in the world. According to the famous Dr. Frank Tallis, who studied this disease, the love affliction should also attract the attention of representatives of clinical medicine in the modern world.

However, not all figures of modern science are so categorically and negatively. Helen Fisher, a well-known US anthropologist, put forward a very bold theory some time ago. She believes that love, including unrequited love, is primarily a natural factor in evolution, and the stress it accompanies helps a person develop and improve.

Fisher continued her research on romantic love and its implications for human evolution for more than 10 years and came to several conclusions. Firstly, she is convinced that it is the ability to love that gives a person the strength to live and develop, makes his existence interesting. Second, the anthropologist assures his followers that the ability and desire to love "has a profound effect on our social and genetic future."After studying the mechanism of human love for a long time, Helen came to the conclusion that it is nothing more than an "evolutionary adaptation."The anthropologist believes that "the ability to fall in love has evolved because those who focus their efforts on wooing one preferential person save time and energy, and increase their survival and reproductive rates."

As for unrequited love, she expressed herself even more categorically: “Unfortunately, the same applies to the dark side of a great feeling. For sound evolutionary reasons, we are designed to suffer terribly from rejection by someone we adore.”

Helen Fisher, famous for her progressive views, believes that stress is nothing more than a kind of evolutionary mechanism of self-defense against romantic experiences, both negative and positive. In the human brain, the areas responsible for hate and love are located close to each other and are closely connected; and it is to this connection that a person owes his ability to quickly replace love with hate in times of great stress, and then begin the process of finding a new potential partner.

Supporting the point of view of a number of modern doctors regarding the strong indifference of stress and romantic experiences, Helen Fisher nevertheless argues that pain, anger and despair can still bring more benefit than harm. "Cruel depression can push us to realize the bitter truth and make difficult decisions. And this contributes to our success in survival and reproduction," Fisher concluded.

Computer stress

Modern information technologies add to

– loss of information;

– computer malfunctions;

– information overload;

– slow operation of the information system;

– spam;

– A program with an unfriendly or hidden interface.

Loss of information is one of the main causes of stress. A computer freeze in itself is a considerable stress, but if the hard drive breaks down, and, accordingly, all the important data stored on it is destroyed, the health of the person working with it is seriously tested. People with a weakened nervous system can be in danger of a nervous breakdown, and with a sick heart - a heart attack. There is a known case when an engineer of a large company, who was fulfilling an important order, lost all the collected information as a result of a hard drive failure and became a victim of severe stress, began to suffocate from an attack of sudden asthma.

You can lose data not only because of a hard drive failure. A virus that has entered an electronic system, or the pranks of inexperienced users can erase some of the information, or even completely upset the computer. Statistics show that every day thousands of people lose important data on their hard drive: articles, dissertations, theses, abstracts, reports, etc. It is easy to imagine how this affects their state of mind and health.

Even if computer problems do not lead to the loss of information, they are still powerful stressors. In the life of any PC user or programmer, there have been cases when the "mechanical inquisitor" refused to install the necessary program or interfered with working with your favorite game.

In the age of computer technology, there is a problem of redundant information. The Internet and the abundance of various programs force people to constantly improve their skills and expand their knowledge. Not everyone is able to do this. People who are trying to work with a lot of information often cannot cope with the load and experience long term stress.

When irritating factors accumulate, and a person does not see a way out of this situation, a spontaneous emotional explosion can occur. This kind of computer stress is very dangerous because it is very difficult to overcome. The affected person may quickly develop some kind of mental or nervous disease. There are cases when people who spent most of their lives near the monitor went crazy or plunged into a deep depression.

About 90% of users regularly experience stress when encountering computer problems, and the loss of time spent identifying and fixing those causes even more irritation. Important work that a person does not have time to complete in a quality and timely manner due to incorrect PC operation is far from the only reason for dissatisfaction. A system failure while watching a movie, playing a game or accessing the Internet can piss off the most patient and accommodating person. However, there are also those who believe that computers are simply not worth being nervous about.

Unfortunately, there are not many such personalities - only 7% of users.

The reaction of a person who encounters problems with a computer is very typical. Approximately 40% of users will start swearing loudly, hitting the keys and the system unit with their fists. Another 40%, with irritation and panic, will try to find out and fix the cause of the problems, for which they can call a more experienced person. The most mature 17% will take the problem for granted and patiently set about fixing it. And only 3% of programmers and hackers will consider the situation interesting, consider it a challenge to themselves, and will be happy to study it.

Programs with an unfriendly or hidden interface are also a major source of stress. The interface is designed to exchange information between the user and the program. It includes various codes, command modes, formats, devices designed for data input, a method for communicating a computer system with a user, documentation for a program, a navigator, etc.

If the program downloaded to the computer is categorically refuses to communicate with the user, the person, according to experts, experiences the same pain and shock as from a punch to the solar plexus.

It is especially unpleasant for the user to encounter programs designed in such a way as to limit their communication with a person. This so-called black box principle, in which the user does not see how the system reacts to his commands and whether it responds to them at all, greatly undermines the mental health of a person.

Rest stress

Many psychologists are sure that rest from work exceeding 1 week is very unhealthy. Some time ago, in

Spain, scientists conducted research, during which they found that more than 35% of people returning from vacation to a normal mode of existence, that is, to the workplace, experience severe stress.

Most likely, this problem is a consequence of the fact that people who go on vacation are not psychologically ready to stop it. On a subconscious level, they believe that there is still time before the end of the vacation, and its actual completion is met with a wave of surprise, indignation and longing. That is, according to an article published in one of the issues of the Izvestia newspaper, "... the shorter the vacation, the less likely it is to fall into depression upon returning home."

Exam Stress

Exam stress is one of the most common in the world. Recent studies conducted by American scientists have shown that during the pre-examination period, 60% of applicants and students have significantly increased blood pressure, and anxiety and malnutrition contribute to weight loss in another 48%.

Examinees constantly experience stress, suffer from nausea and headaches, diarrhea and skin diseases, feel a general decline in strength, and feel constant fear. Their self-criticism increases significantly, complexes intensify, sleep and memory are disturbed, and appetite either worsens or grows.

People suffering from exam stress are constantly tormented by memories of past failures, both their own and those of others. During the exam, their blood pressure rises or falls sharply, sweating becomes more intense, and breathing is frequent. Panic attacks overload the brain and nervous system, causing intense stress and causing fainting and memory lapses.

Experts believe that exam stress is the result of excessive mental stress, increasing stress on certain muscles during the study of the material and, most importantly, fear. Panic is the main cause of this kind of stress.

Stress and the body

For quite a long time, scientists have noticed that a person's resistance to various diseases depends on his personal qualities. It is also no secret that the cause of physical ailments, as a rule, is mental problems.

Today, many people already know that the human body is gradually changing under the influence of psychological factors. There are many examples of this: for example, strong negative emotions can cause the early appearance of gray hair, an abundance of stress - stooping, love unrest - malfunctions of the cardiovascular system, problems in personal life -

insomnia and loss of appetite, fear - diabetes.

Not always stress is accompanied by obvious symptoms. Much more often, nervous tension affects the state of human muscle tissue. This was first noticed a very long time ago and confirmed by the observations of many famous scientists of antiquity, such as Hippocrates, who once said that the diagnosis of diseases should begin with observing the behavior of the patient, and not with a conversation with him. The way a person walks, sits down, stands up, moves his arms and tilts his head can tell a lot to an experienced specialist.

Stress causes strong muscle tension, as if preparing them to protect themselves from adverse factors. But since the possibility of physical suppression of the threat does not always exist and this is far from the best way to solve the problem, it is often not possible to relieve the resulting muscle tension.

Accumulating, internal tension provokes the so-called muscle clamp, which intensifies over time under the influence of subsequent stresses. By observing a person, you can determine which muscle group was most affected by stress. The stiffness of movements will speak for itself, and an experienced specialist will be able to understand what he should pay attention to and what exactly causes stress in the patient.

Muscle clamp is not always as harmless as it might seem at first glance. It often causes the development of radiculitis, lameness, nervous spasms, headaches, nervous tics, convulsions, coordination disorders, dysfunctions of the musculoskeletal system, and cardiovascular diseases.

Below are some of the most common muscle clamps, which, when turned into a chronic form, can cause the development of the above diseases. The most probable causes that caused such a stress reaction are given.

1. Clamping the muscles of the shoulder girdle and neck. Causes stoop, in the future it can lead to a curvature of the spine and a violation of posture. It is caused by stress, which is caused by problems in personal life that a person cannot cope with on his own.

2. Clamping the muscles in the back. It leads to sciatica and provokes disturbances in the functioning of the musculoskeletal system. The causes of occurrence may be different. The most typical are problems in personal life, too much emotional and physical stress.

3. Muscle contraction in the abdomen. Often occurs when a person is afraid for his life. The patient begins to hunch over, as if covering the vulnerable area with his hands. His gait becomes uneven, and his movements are uncertain. The development of such a muscle clamp can lead to a violation of the functions of the digestive organs.

4. Clamping of the muscles in the neck. A person constantly pulls his head into his shoulders or walks without looking up from the ground. This clamping can cause frequent cramps in the muscles of the neck and shoulders, which appears if the victim has problems communicating with children or dependents. The presence of a burden provokes more and more stress, which is very difficult to get rid of.

5. Clamping of the facial muscles. It occurs in people who try to hide their thoughts and emotions from others, mainly out of fear of being ridiculed. Due to the constant tension of the facial muscles, a kind of facial distortion or convulsions may occur. In a neglected state, the clamp can provoke progressive spasms of the facial muscles and a nervous tic.

6. Clamping the muscles of the legs. A clamp on the anterior thigh can occur when a person feels the desire to break off a relationship with someone

as soon as possible.

This unfulfilled desire leads to gradually growing tension in the muscles. Constant self-doubt, in one's own strengths and actions, the feeling that there is no reliable support can cause clamping of the calf muscles.

Unstable family relationships, inflation, in general, abrupt changes in life are often manifested by the clamping of the muscles of the external surface of the thigh.

7. Clamp of the gluteal muscles. It develops in people who fear punishment. May indicate that the person is suffering from feelings of insecurity.

Therapeutic nutrition for stress

The human diet must be balanced, that is, fully satisfy the body's needs for all the necessary food and essential substances. It is necessary to ensure that the daily diet includes them in proportions that provide optimal interrelationships and a combination of irreplaceable components. True, some believe that the body will still balance the nutrients in its own way, according to its individual needs. This can be confirmed by the participation of amino acids in the synthesis of various substances, which constantly occurs in the body even when the most rational and highly valuable proteins are taken with food. Combinations and complexes that arc provided for by a balanced diet. There are other, less significant objections. However, a balanced diet for most age categories is, apparently, the most acceptable and complete.

Food should be not only high-calorie, but also biologically complete. To do this, you need to eat more vegetables, fruits, as well as food and wild greens. Parsley, dill, green onions, cilantro, watercress, mint and other herbs are very useful for the prevention of atherosclerosis, neurosis, and stress.

These products should become a mandatory component of the diet.

It is recommended to choose coarse grains, as they contain more fiber and nutrients. You can increase your intake of fresh fruits and vegetables, as well as foods rich in fiber. It is best to avoid overly salty foods.

You need to eat 3 times a day, without depleting the body with a minimum amount of calories. If a person runs or swims long distances or increases the amount of exercise, his need for food must increase, otherwise the person will suffer from a lack of it, which will lead to a violation of the rational ratio of calories. As a result, the energy resources of the body will decrease, and the person will constantly experience fatigue. Even if he does not feel tired during the day, after dinner he will feel that he was completely exhausted. Intercepting something on the go or forgetting about food, such a person will become irritated on insignificant occasions, it will be difficult for him to concentrate.

You also need to make sure that the menu is varied. It should contain carbohydrates (fruits, vegetables, flour and starchy foods), proteins (meat or dairy products, beans or peas), fats (butter or margarine), and liquids. This will allow a person to be full of energy all day long. Carbohydrates are burned first, providing the body with energy for 3-4 hours. Proteins provide energy for the next 1-2 hours, and fats are not completely wasted after 5 or 6 hours, that is, until the next meal.

Carbohydrates

About 50% of calories consumed daily should come from foods containing carbohydrates. They energize the body, contain many minerals and vitamins important for health, and fibers that promote good digestion and reduce the likelihood of bowel cancer. In addition, most carbohydrate foods contain a lot of water.

The combination of water and fiber creates a volume of food that gives a feeling of fullness, preventing overeating. At the same time, the number of calories is relatively low. For example, a small orange or apple contains only 50 kcal, while a potato tuber or a slice of bread contains 70 kcal. You can compare these low-calorie foods with steak (800 kcal) or sweet caramel (200 kcal).

Carbohydrates form the basis of such foods as fruits, juices, fresh vegetables, beans, peas, lentils, potatoes, corn, whole meal bread, as well as porridge made from whole oats, brown rice and bran.

Squirrels

Foods containing proteins provide the body with energy resources that will be put into action when carbohydrates are burned. Protein foods should make up about 20% of your daily calories. These include fish, poultry, veal, lean beef, lamb, pork, cheese, milk, cottage cheese, yogurt, eggs, dry peas, and beans.

It is recommended to eat mainly lean beef, lamb and pork. It is better to choose cheeses, milk and yogurt with the lowest fat content. Also useful are fish, poultry and veal, which contain many valuable trace elements.

Fats

When choosing this type of product, you need to pay attention not only to quantity, but also to quality. Vegetable fats found in corn oil, margarine, mayonnaise, salad dressings, nuts, and seeds, preferable to animals, which are abundant in butter, sour cream, whole milk products, fatty meats and bacon.

It is better to eat less fatty foods,

that is, limit the use of fried meat, butter, margarine, mayonnaise, vegetable oil, sauces, nuts, canned food, semi-finished products, fatty meat products (bacon, sausage, roast beef, sausages, stewed beef, lamb, pork), high-fat dairy products (whole milk, cream, sour cream, cheese, ice cream).

It is recommended to use vegetable margarine, as it contains more polyunsaturated fats than regular margarine. Butter is better to prefer vegetable. Fats are necessary for the body, as they contribute to a longer preservation of the feeling of satiety and reduce thirst. In addition, dietary fats inhibit insulin secretion, stimulate the production of enzymes that break down fats in the body, which leads to their more intensive consumption.

You should not try to make food more high-calorie. People engaged in mental labor, workers of automated and highly mechanized industrial enterprises, people of mature, elderly and retirement age do not need a plentiful fatty diet at all.

It used to be believed that animal fats are more complete than vegetable fats. However, this is not so: the study of the properties of vegetable oils revealed the presence in their composition of a number of biologically valuable components that are absent in animal fats, including butter. For example, such substances necessary for the body as essential unsaturated fatty acids, sterols, phosphatides, tocopherol, necessary for the normalization of fat metabolism in the body, turned out to be in greater quantities in vegetable oils. Their biological action to a certain extent is aimed at preventing the development of atherosclerosis. Along with this, the negative properties of the predominant consumption of animal fats were revealed. Thus, animal fats today fade into the background, and vegetable fats are strongly recommended.

However, you should not completely exclude animal fats. The biological usefulness of fat is ensured only when fats of both vegetable and animal origin are included in it, which mutually complement each other with the missing components. Eating only vegetable oil deprives the body of

Many vital substances (contained, in particular, in butter). Vegetable oil should be included in the diet daily in small quantities (approximately 20–25 g).Useful margarine is a combined fat that combines vegetable and animal fats. It can be fortified in various ways, milk and cream can be introduced into it, fat from fish and marine animals can be used.

Vitamins

Vitamins play an indispensable role in rational nutrition - biologically highly active substances that improve the internal environment of the body, increasing the functional ability of its main systems and resistance to the action of adverse external and internal factors. By improving the state of the internal environment, vitamins increase the body's resistance to disease. That is why they should be considered as an important means of general primary prevention of diseases. Thanks to vitamins, overall performance increases, the aging process of the body slows down. The lack of vitamins leads to the development of atherosclerosis, peroxidation, neuroses, stress conditions, etc.

Manifestations of vitamin deficiency often do not occur in isolation, in the form of an independent, specific, pronounced symptom complex, but mainly in combination with any type of modern pathology, contributing to its development and aggravating, complicating the course of the disease. Vitamin deficiency is a factor complicating the course of coronary heart disease and rehabilitation after myocardial infarction.

Products that help fight stress

Some foods, such as sugar, honey, fruits and vegetables, are essential for the body to deal with stress. However, you should not abuse them, as this can backfire and create additional problems with digestion.

Sugar

Sugar is a valuable, easily digestible food product. In the body, it is used to form glycogen, a substance that nourishes the liver, heart, and muscles. It is an obligatory component of the blood, where its amount is maintained at a constant level. However, with its abundant use, the formation of fat in the body from other nutrients sharply increases.Eating too much sugar has a negative effect on the state of beneficial intestinal microflora. There is evidence that excess sugar contributes to metabolic disorders and the development of atherosclerosis.

It's no secret that foods containing sugar can quickly lift your mood or help you cope with stress, but you should still eat them in limited quantities, especially refined sugar. It is found in foods such as jam, jelly, lemonade, dessert sweets, hard candies, homemade cookies, pies, sweet juices, and canned fruits.

Honey

Honey is included in the group of especially active food products. It is difficult to compare any other food product with it both in terms of the number of constituent components and biological properties. Even products as actively expressed in biological terms as sea buckthorn, magnolia vine, eleuthero coccus, are inferior to honey in terms of the versatility of their biological and therapeutic effects.

A distinctive feature of honey is precisely the variety its biological action and versatility of healing properties.

Honey is, first of all, an unsurpassed normalizer of many initial disorders and disorders of the healthy state of the body and its individual systems. The importance of honey as a remedy widely used in folk medicine in the treatment of colds is well known. No less widely known was honey and as a light sedative.

Honey has long been referred to as an unsurpassed restorative and tonic agent for various kinds of exhaustion, weakening after an illness, and for restoring various body functions. The role of honey in overwork is exceptionally great. There is evidence of its favorable effect in neuro psychic overload and stressful conditions. The successful use of honey for the treatment of peptic ulcer of the stomach and duodenum, as well as gastritis and other diseases of the digestive system is known. If we collect all the available information about the beneficial properties of honey, then its high value will become even more obvious not only as a food product, but also as a healing tool in the fight against stress.

Honey is the nectar of flowers processed by bees into food. The color, aroma and taste of honey depend on the plants from which the bees collect nectar: from fireweed, alfalfa or sweet clover - colorless, from white acacia light yellow, from sunflower - yellow, from buckwheat, heather or sage- yellow-brown, from buckwheat dark brown.

Important components of honey are organic acids (lactic, malic, citric, oxalic) and enzymes (diastase, catalase, inverses, lipase, phosphatase).Royal jelly mixed with honey is widely used for neuro psychic overload, neurosis, irritability, stressful conditions, general overwork, asthenia, insomnia, premature old age, liver damage, gout, etc.

Vegetables

It's good to eat more low-calorie, bulky, high-fiber foods, such as raw fruits and vegetables (with seeds and skins), boiled potatoes, whole meal breads, bran, roasted corn, and lean soups.

Vegetables can be eaten raw, steamed, baked. However, one should not forget that heat treatment significantly reduces the content of vitamins and mineral components. Vegetables and fruits stimulate digestion and the absorption of proteins and carbohydrates.

Sterols of vegetables and fruits inhibit the conversion of carbohydrates into fats. In addition, vegetables and fruits are an important source of vitamins, mineral salts and organic acids necessary for metabolism.

Beverages

To successfully combat stress, it is recommended to limit alcohol consumption. In addition, alcoholic beverages, including beer, increase appetite and contribute to overeating.

Drink 6-8 glasses daily liquids, preferably water. Useful skimmed milk, saturated with vitamins A and D, natural fruit juices, mineral water. Under stress, it is recommended to limit (up to 2-3 times a day) the consumption of drinks containing caffeine (tea, coffee, Coca-Cola, Pepsi-Cola).

Food intake

It is necessary to eat slowly, relaxed, in a calm, pleasant environment. It is desirable to create an appropriate atmosphere for this. You need to chew food thoroughly and spend at least 20 minutes for each meal.

You should adhere to a rational diet. You need to eat regularly - this will avoid the influence of unforeseen circumstances (for example, Sunday and holiday meals). In order to for the prevention of stressful conditions, they take food 4-5 times a day in small portions, and for the treatment of stress 5-6 times a day. This achieves a decrease in the feeling of hunger and an increase in energy consumption for the assimilation of the food taken. Most of the food should be consumed in the morning. The intervals between meals should not exceed 4 hours. Dinner should be no later than 3 hours before bedtime. After dinner, you can go for a walk or do some work associated with a little physical activity.

It is better to limit the intake of sodium salts, which can lead to an increase in blood pressure. To do this, add to foodless salt, less likely to eat various pickles, canned beef, pork, sausages, ham, bacon, sausages, cheese, convenience foods, snacks, canned soups and vegetables, sauces. Make soups with homemade broth or opt for low-sodium concentrates.

It is better to avoid unnecessary

thoughts about food. It is recommended to store food out of sight so that there is no temptation to snack.

Food should be served on the table in the required quantity, and not on large dishes. It is not advisable to combine food with watching TV, reading or other activities.

It is advisable to learn how to cope with stress without resorting to food or alcohol. Overeating and drinking are all too often associated with everyday anxieties or the need to unwind after a busy day at work. But there are other ways for this, for example, physical exercises, autogenic training.

Biologically active additives

"Live greens plus" (Vita Green Plus)

This is one of the Cambridge Nutrition dietary supplements, which is a special concentrated nutrient mixture of food herbs and algae. "Live greens plus" is an effective means of preventing cancer.

It consists of the following components: various types of edible algae (brown, blue-green, dark red, chlorella, and spirulina); powder from the greens of germinated seeds of barley, wheat, oats; cabbage, parsley, spinach, broccoli, celery, alfalfa, nettle, dandelion, thistle; natural enzymes bromelain and papaya; nutrient medium for their reproduction.

fructooligosaccharides;acidophilic bacteria - lactospores;

– acerola.Action taken:

– increases resistance to stress and adverse environmental conditions;

– increases efficiency and vitality;

– has antiatherosclerotic action;

– restores and maintains normal intestinal flora;

– prevents decay processes;

– promotes purification and removal of harmful substances;

– enhances peristalsis intestines, improves the functioning of the secretory organs of the gastric tract;

– normalizes the functions of the immune and endocrine systems;

– Prevents the development of cancer, mas to pithy; has a general health effect.

Recommendations for use: 1 teaspoon diluted in water or juice. Consume 30 minutes before meals 3 times a day. After preparation, the mixture is stored in the refrigerator without freezing.

Contraindications: "Living greens plus" is not recommended for acute diseases of the gastrointestinal tract, intestinal obstruction and in the period after surgical operations on the organs of the digestive system.

It is recommended to store the drug in a dark, cool place. Approved for use by the Ministry of Health of the Russian Federation.

"Natural Energizer" (Natural Enerigizer)

This is a natural food supplement that restores the energy resources of the body.

It contains: 300 mg of guarana extract, 100 mg of pollen, 60 mg of kola nut, 25 mg of gotu kola, and 25 mg of schisandra.

Action taken:

– catabolic action, including increased breakdown of fats and proteins;

– adapt genic effect, increasing the body's defenses and general tonic effect (schizandra and kola nut);

– soothing and stress-relieving effect without inhibiting higher nervous activity, but, on the contrary, improving mental abilities and sharpness of thinking (gotu kola);

– stimulation of cardiovascular activity due to the action caffeine contained in guarana;

– Stimulating the immune system and improving nutrition

Suggested Use: Take 1 to 3 capsules per day. Food. Pox

Therapeutic and prophylactic food supplement company "Vision".

The composition includes lemon balm, lavender, palaver rocks, magnesium, and complex

vitaminsAT.

Action taken:

– relieves stress, eliminates the feeling of fear, protects against neuroses;

– reducesthe weight;

– Promotes the removal of heavy metals from

Purpose:

– indicated for bronchitis, respiratory infections, psychosis and psoriasis;

– Recommended for spasms of the stomach and intestines,

Not addictive.

It is recommended for drivers, students during exams, surgeons during surgery, as well as for everyone during hard work and stressful situations.

Used as a daytime tranquilizer without dulling the reaction with absolute concentration on daily activities.

Suggested Use: Take 1 capsule in the morning and evening with a glass of water, preferably with a meal.

Chapter 2

The nervous system and pathological changes in it

As you know, the human nervous system, unlike all others, is responsible for the coordinated work of all systems and organs necessary to maintain the vital activity of a healthy organism as a whole. The nervous system controls and coordinates all processes in the body. In addition, it is responsible for the direct contact of the organism with the environment (perception, processing and reproduction of the information received).

The intermediary between the body and the external environment is the nervous tissue through which impulses pass to the nervous system, due to which this or that information is perceived in a special way (smells, sounds, tangible objects). This main structural component of the nervous system consists of two types of cells - neurons (they conduct nerve impulses to the brain and perform the function of excitation) and gliocytes (they perform supporting, trophic and protective functions).

The human nervous system is divided into central and peripheral, as well as somatic and autonomic.

The central nervous system consists of the brain and spinal cord. As you know, the brain is located in the cranium. The brain consists of lobes that perform various functions, but in general they all come down to the perception, processing and reproduction of information received from the environment. The spinal cord is a strand of brain tissue located in the spinal canal. This department of the nervous system performs several functions: first of all, it is a conductive function, which is carried out by the so-called ascending conductors, which are responsible for assessing the position of the body in space (joint-muscular feeling), as well as controlling the reflex activity of the body, for example, tendon knee jerk.

In addition to the central nervous system, the peripheral nervous system is also known. It is a collection of spinal (31 pairs) and cranial (12 pairs) nerves. The work of these nerves is carried out in concert, from the spinal cord and brain to the periphery. This group of nerves helps the body in one way or another to respond to external impulses, and they are divided into several species, for example, visual, olfactory, oculomotor, and vague and others.

The autonomic nervous system is responsible for nutrition, excretion, reproduction, respiration, circulation of fluids in the body.

The somatic nervous system is a collection of sensory nerve fibers that innervate muscles and joints in the human body. In other words, this section of the nervous system performs its functions due to impulses coming from the higher section of the central nervous system, which controls all systems of the body as a whole. For example, if a person is frightened or in danger, he will intuitively act to save his life. At this time, the following happens in the body at the level of the central nervous system: impulses that suddenly arise in impulses very quickly go from the brain to the peripheral parts, namely, to the somatic nervous system. Due to this, certain muscles necessary for a person to carry out specific body movements are innervated.

In modern medicine, there is a unified classification of diseases of the nervous system, compiled according to the principle of influence and impact on the central nervous system of such factors as trauma (various fractures, electrical injuries, etc.), heredity, and complications after serious illnesses, etc. The listed reasons are the main ones, since one way or another they affect the occurrence and development of a particular disease of the nervous system.

Since almost all diseases of the central nervous system proceed and are treated quite difficult, in many cases the nutrition of patients requires compliance with special diets. Many doctors consider the preparation of certain diets for such patients to be quite difficult, which is associated with the severe course of nervous diseases.

This book presents some diseases of the nervous system, the treatment of which requires the observance of special diets, which contributes to the gradual recovery of the patient or the improvement of his general condition.

Separately, there are diseases associated with a disorder of the human psyche. In general, mental disorders are pathological in nature, but have not been fully investigated. The main causes of such diseases are complications after previous diseases. Various kinds (infectious, hereditary, acquired), as well as with cranial cerebral injuries. Therefore, all mental illnesses can be given the following definition: these are diseases caused by disruption of the brain and having a complex character.

Among mental diseases, there are those that arise and develop due to other reasons: these are hereditary diseases (for example, hemophilia), psycho-emotional instability of a person (hysteria), and the social factor (drug addiction) also has an influence to a certain extent.

All mental disorders and diseases to some extent have a severe course and, as a result, are difficult to treat. All patients suffering from mental disorders, in any case, are under the supervision of a psychotherapist, who prescribes a special course of treatment that is individual in nature.

Thus, in general, the nervous system is a single complex, the work of which is carried out in a coordinated and, accordingly, sequentially (for a specific situation). In addition, since the brain is the center of the nervous system, all the processes occurring in it (including pathological ones) are very difficult to control by a person.

Chapter 3
Characteristics of the main diseases of the central nervous system and therapeutic nutrition for them

The most common diseases of the central nervous system include adiposogenital dystrophy, arachoiditis, ataxia, cerebral atherosclerosis, migraine, etc.

Adiposogenital dystrophy

This is a disease characterized by signs of a violation of the hypothalamic-pituitary symptom complex.

This disease is characterized by gradually increasing obesity. In this case, fat deposits are observed on the shoulders, mammary glands (regardless of the patient's gender), abdomen, thighs and buttocks. This pathological obesity occurs due to the slowing down of the gonads. In patients, there is a decrease in potency (in men) and the phenomenon of amenorrhea (in women).

In cases where the disease began in childhood, patients experience growth retardation, while secondary sexual characteristics either develop insufficiently or disappear altogether. At the same time, the uterus does not develop in women or infertility is recorded.

As a rule, the temperature in patients with this disease is low. These symptoms are the result of disruption of the endocrine system and the metabolic system.

Treatment

In the treatment of this disease, the main thing is the fight against morbid obesity in patients. To do this, the course of treatment includes dietary nutrition, which is based on the use of products containing the least amount of animal fats. Here you can use mainly vegetable products: apples, turnips, beets, turnips, cranberries, cabbage, spinach, lettuce, carrots. In addition, doctors advise to consume more berry juices.

Fasting days

Fasting days will help you quickly lose weight. They can be carried out 1-2 times a week. By composition, fasting days are divided into:

– Carbohydrate (apple, watermelon, cucumber, etc.);

– fat (sour cream or cream);

– protein (meat, cottage cheese, kefir, fish);

– combined (complex).

When choosing a fasting day, it is recommended to focus on the tastes and habits of the patient, however, it is best to start the treatment of this disease from a meat, cottage cheese or sour cream day, as they are easier to tolerate by the body, and are not inferior in effectiveness to others. If the patient tolerates hunger well, then to enhance the therapeutic effect you can try to spend double fasting days.

During carbohydrate fasting days, it is necessary to limit the intake of proteins and fats. Choose products that contain complex carbohydrates, vegetable fiber, vitamins, mineral salts: unsweetened apples, fresh cucumbers, watermelons, tomatoes, plums, cherries, currants and other vegetables and fruits. During the day, at regular intervals in 5 doses, you should consume 1,500 kg of any of these products in raw form. Additional fluid intake during fasting days is usually not recommended, since the products used contain a sufficient amount of water.

Fat fasting days stimulate the activity of enzymes that break down fats, inhibit the transition of carbohydrates into fats and create rest for the overexcited insulin-producing apparatus of the pancreas of an obese patient. On this day, 500 g of 20% sour cream or cream should be consumed in 5 equal portions at regular intervals. Twice a day it is recommended to drink 1 glass of rosehip infusion or coffee with milk without sugar.

Protein fasting days are easier than others. Thanks to them, metabolism improves and the activity of enzymes that destroy fats increases. Recommended cottage cheese (150 g with 15 g of sour cream 4 times a day) or kefir (250 ml 6 times a day). Twice a day you can drink 1 glass of coffee with milk (50 ml) without sugar or with sorbitol.

Meat fasting days are quite effective. During the day, it is recommended to eat 450 g of boiled lean meat, dividing it into 5 servings. Three times a day they drink 1 glass of coffee with milk without sugar or with sorbitol (xylitol) and 2 glasses of rosehip infusion.

On combined fasting days, it is recommended to use different combinations of products. For example, a rice-apple day diet consists of 3 servings of rice porridge (25 g of rice and 150 ml of milk for each serving) and 800-1000 g of raw or baked apples. When combining cottage cheese with curdled milk, take 3 servings of cottage cheese, 150 g each (you can cook cottage cheese) and 3 servings of curdled milk, 200–250 g each. It is recommended to combine products that are similar in chemical composition, such as meat and fish, vegetables and fruits, vegetables and berries, etc. P.

If 2 unloading days are used in a

row, then it is better to spend the 1st meat day, and the 2nd - sour cream or vegetable day. As a result, body weight can decrease by 2–2.5 kg.

On fasting days, it is recommended to engage in ordinary physical or mental work, which distracts from thoughts about food. food is better taken separately from other family members. Night sleep during unloading should be extended to 9 hours. It is desirable to control the effectiveness of the unloading day by weighing.

Unloading week

Against the background of this diet, you cannot drink alcoholic beverages, as this will disrupt the process of removing fat from the body. Drinking alcohol is allowed only 24 hours after the end of the diet. The main thing in this diet is soup for weight loss, which you need to eat daily several times a day as much as you want. The more the patient eats, the more weight will be lost.

With strict adherence to the diet for a week, you can get rid of 5-9 kg. It is very important that those foods that are recommended by the diet are eaten exactly on the days they need to be eaten. If during the week the patient has lost 7 or more kg, it is better to take a break from the diet for 2 days. You can continue it at any time. But you should not eat soup outside the diet.

You can use the diet as often as you like. If it was interrupted, you need to start again from the first day.

Soup for weight loss

Ingredients: 6 medium onions, a few (to taste) tomatoes (canned), 1 small head of cabbage, 2 green peppers, 1 bunch of celery, 1 vegetable stock cube, curry or hot sauce to taste.

Cooking method

Cut vegetables into small or medium pieces and cover with water. Season with salt, pepper, optional curry or hot sauce. Boil over high heat for 10 minutes, then reduce the heat and continue to cook until the vegetables are soft.

You should not eat exclusively this soup. The diet must be supplemented with other components.

First day Eat soup and any fruit except bananas. They drink tea or coffee without sugar and milk, cranberry juice and water.

Second day Eat soup, as well as fresh or canned vegetables and herbs. It is necessary to exclude only dried legumes, green peas and corn. During lunch, you can eat a baked potato with butter. Fruit should not be eaten. They only drink water.

Third day Eat soup, fruits and vegetables (excluding baked potatoes, bananas and legumes), drink water. In three days the patient should lose 2 to 3 kg.

Fourth day Eat soup, fruits and vegetables, including bananas (no more 3 pcs.), drink skimmed milk and water.

Fifth day Soup, beef (300-600 g per day) and tomatoes (fresh or canned) are eaten. Drink 6-8 glasses of water.

Sixth day Eat beef, vegetables (especially leafy) and soup, drink water. You shouldn't eat baked potatoes.

Seventh day

Eat brown rice, unsweetened fruit juice, vegetables, and soup.

Can be added to soup or vegetables any spices. They only drink water.

During the fasting week, you should not eat bread, alcohol, carbonated (effervescent) drinks.

Nothing should be fried or cooked with fat added.

During the unloading week, you must adhere to the following rules:

– do not deviate from the menu, do not add any other products;

– weigh yourself in the morning;

– eat soup every time there will be a feeling of hunger;

– use oil only once a week with baked potatoes;

– Carefully cut off all the fat from the meat, remove the skin from the bird.

In addition to diets, which are symptomatic treatment and are aimed solely at weight loss, antibiotics and urotropin are prescribed. For tumors, radiation therapy and surgery are indicated.

With bulimia, patients are prescribed

drugs depimon, teronak.

With a decrease in thyroid function, its hormones and diuretics are indicated. Enter chorionic gonadotropin 1000-1500 IU 2 times a week for 2 months with a break of 2-3 weeks.

In the absence of the effect of the ongoing treatment, patients who have reached the age of 14–15 years and have underdevelopment of the genital organs are prescribed sex hormones.

Boys are shown methyl testosterone 5 mg 3 times a day, testosterone propionate 1 ml of a 5% solution intramuscularly 2-3 times a week for 2 months, teste Nat - 1 ml of a 10% solution 1 time in 2 weeks intramuscularly (10 injections), sustanon-250 1 ml intramuscularly once a month for 6-12 months.

Girls are prescribed estrogens (microfollin, sinestrol and other drugs) for 15-20 days, then a course of progesterone or pregnin for 8-10 days.

Arachnoiditis

The name of this disease is from the Greek word translated "spider". This name was given to the disease because arachnoiditis is an inflammation of the arachnoid membrane of the brain, which covers it from the outside with the thinnest network of vessels and formations from various kinds of connective tissue. Arachnoiditis develops as a result of an infectious lesion of the arachnoid membrane of the brain. This disease can occur as a complication after meningitis or traumatic brain injury.

Most often, arachnoiditis is preceded by an infectious disease. The incubation period is 10-12 days.

The disease is accompanied by severe headaches (bursting or pressing), especially in the eye area. It is for this reason that patients cannot sleep at night, their working capacity decreases, and their vision deteriorates noticeably.

Women suffer from arachnoiditis, as a rule, more often than men.

The disease is very difficult to recognize, because it has a blurred symptomatology. Even with the use of modern methods of examination, it is quite difficult to accurately establish the diagnosis. Despite this, arachnoiditis is considered a common disease that can cause hypochondria and various kinds of neurotic disorders.

Health food

It should be said that the treatment of arachnoiditis is carried out on an outpatient basis. In this case, the patient is recommended to visit a psychotherapist. This is due to the fact that after this diagnosis is made by a doctor, many patients fall into a deep depression. At the same time, they feel disabled (even apply for a disability), because they believe that they have developed an organic brain lesion that cannot be cured by anything. In such cases, patients are immersed in their own microcosm and live only with thoughts about their illness.

That is why the attending physician needs to explain as soon as possible that such patients should lead a full-fledged lifestyle. The only condition may be such a choice of profession, type of activity that could contribute to the recovery of the patient (in such cases, doctors advice to be in the fresh air more often, do light worked.).

The course of treatment of patients with arachnoiditis includes the intake of B vitamins, as well as vasodilators and absorbable drugs. In addition, as a sedative, doctor's recommend using the Manchurian aralia, which helps to remove the patient from a depressive state.

It should be noted that patients with arachnoiditis retain their working capacity and significant vital activity, although the possibility of complete recovery is very doubtful.

Tincture of Aralia Manchurian roots

The tincture is prepared in a 70% alcohol solution or vodka in a ratio of 20 g of roots per 10 ml of alcohol. A 20% tincture, the action of which is similar to ginseng, is taken 30–40 drops 3 times a day as a tonic for impotence.

There is another option, when the tincture is prepared in a 70% alcohol solution in the ratio of 1 part of the roots to 5 parts of alcohol and take 10-15 drops per dose 2 times a day.

Foods rich in B vitamins

With arachnoiditis, it is recommended to eat more foods rich in B vitamins.

Liver. It contains vitamins B2, PP,

pantothenic acid, B6, choline, B12. It can be consumed boiled or stewed.

Kidneys. It should be noted that the specific taste and smell of kidney dishes are a significant obstacle to their widespread daily use in nutrition.

Bakery products. Since vitamins are concentrated in the germ and shells of the grain, the coarser the bread that retains these elements, the richer it is in vitamins. To increase the content of B vitamins in bread and bakery products, vitaminization of flour of the highest grades. This made it possible to significantly enrich bread products with vitamins B1, B2 and PP. Products made from fortified flour contain about 3 times more vitamin B1 than non-vitaminized ones, 4-5 times more vitamin B2 and about 2 times more vitamin PP. Thus, for the most complete satisfaction of the need for B vitamins, it is necessary to use bread and bakery products from fortified flour. Currently, the range of such products is quite wide.

Beekeeping products. These include not only honey, but also pollen, apilak (royal jelly), etc. Contraindications to the use of these products can only be an individual intolerance. However, you should not consume honey and other bee products in large quantities, as this can lead to the development of allergies.

Ataxia

The name of this disease in Greek means “mess". This name is directly related to the fact that ataxia is a disease characterized by impaired coordination of movements, one of the most common motor disorders. Ataxia occurs due to damage to the frontal lobes of the brain and cerebellum, as well as deep sensory pathways that are located in the brain and spinal cord.

There are several types of ataxia. Vestibular ataxia affects the frontal part of the brain, in particular, the vestibular apparatus, and can be static and dynamic, cerebellar, sensitive. But all of these species have the same symptoms.

As you know, many parts of the nervous system are responsible for human movements. A healthy person, in the absence of any pathology in the coordination of movements, clearly feels all his movements. However, he is free to control them. All signals coming from the central nervous system are logically interconnected and complement each other. With any damage to certain areas of the brain responsible for the coordination of movements, coordination of movements is disturbed while standing (static ataxia) or when moving (dynamic ataxia).

If a person is sick with ataxia, then while walking, he strongly bends his legs at the knee and hip joints, which is noticeable from the side. At the same time, the patient lowers his legs with great force, such a gait is called punching. Many patients with ataxia complain that they walk as if on cotton wool or a soft surface. Since the patient with ataxia must constantly control his gait, he has to strain his eyesight and look at his feet.

A person with vestibular ataxia experiences constant dizziness, nausea (vomiting is possible). At the same time, it seems to him that all the surrounding objects are moving in a certain direction.

Patients with cerebellar ataxia often lean towards the affected hemisphere and, in the end, unable to maintain balance, fall (most often backwards). In such cases, the patient has a "drunk" gait, he walks awkwardly and sweepingly. A characteristic feature of this disease is the inability of a person to stand with closed eyes. Since the patient with ataxia constantly hands tremble, it is very difficult for him to eat. There are frequent cases of stuttering.

In addition to these symptoms, the diagnosis of "ataxia" is also made with such signs as, for example, deterioration in handwriting. In some cases, the patient cannot thread a needle or even take a match out of a matchbox.

Despite all these symptoms, it is difficult for a doctor to immediately make a correct diagnosis. To clarify and confirm the diagnosis, the doctor usually asks the patient to put his feet together, at the same time close his eyes and stretch his arms forward. In this position, the patient should touch the tip of his nose with his finger. There is also such a way to check the diagnosis for ataxia: the patient should, lying on his back, touch the knee of the other with the heel of one leg. If a person is unable to perform these simple movements, then urgent therapy is required.

Treatment

Usually, with ataxia, the patient is under the direct supervision of a doctor who not only controls the treatment process, but also prescribes a certain diet to the patient, special gymnastic exercises that help restore coordination of movements. The course of treatment also includes the intake of vitamins (especially B vitamins) and restorative agents. About products containing vitamins of group B, described above. You can include them in the diet without restrictions.

Of the drugs in the treatment of this disease, acephen, cerebrolysin, aminalon, piracetam are used. These funds generally affect the metabolism in tissues.

Atherosclerosis of cerebral vessels

Atherosclerosis is a disease of the arteries in which the walls of the arteries harden and thicken due to plaque buildup on the inner walls of the arteries of lipoids (fat-like substances) known as cholesterol. As the layer of cholesterol grows, the gap between the walls of the blood vessels gradually decreases, as a result of which the blood supply is disrupted, and the tissues receive less blood and oxygen coming from the blood.

This disease is a consequence of a violation of lipid metabolism. In addition, the development of the disease is promoted by neuro psychic stress, improper diet (abuse of fatty foods rich in cholesterol), endocrine disorders, hypertension, and smoking. All of these factors take place with the wrong lifestyle.

A patient with atherosclerosis of the cerebral vessels has a decrease in working capacity and an increase in the overall fatigue of the body. At the same time, increased excitability, deterioration of sleep at night and drowsiness during the day are possible. The patient complains of frequent dizziness, severe headaches, and tinnitus. These manifestations of the disease are characteristic of atherosclerosis, which is a consequence of impaired blood supply to the brain. With the development of this disease, a deepening or change in some character traits is possible. For example, a thrifty person becomes stingy, a somewhat sloppy person can become meticulously tidy. Many patients with atherosclerosis have pronounced selfishness.

Along with hypertension, atherosclerosis can be complicated by cerebral hemorrhage, that is, a stroke, often leading to paralysis and even death.

Treatment

During the treatment of patients with atherosclerosis, the correct diet is paramount. At the same time, the attending physician must convince the patient that it is impossible to eat foods that contain cholesterol (eggs, animal fats, meat, sprats, cocoa, chocolate, black tea, sardines, etc.). In addition, it is recommended to increase the intake of vitamin C (ascorbic acid), vitamin B2, which helps to reduce the formation of a layer of cholesterol on the walls of blood vessels, as well as take iodine preparations.

It is known that patients with cerebral atherosclerosis need to eat seaweed containing iodine, peas (vitamin B2), cauliflower, wild strawberries, walnuts, figs, raisins, peeled stewed or fried eggplants (they help reduce blood cholesterol levels, improve metabolism), boiled quince.

With atherosclerosis of the vessels of the brain, doctors advise eating a medium-sized grapefruit every day on an empty stomach, as it prevents the deposition of lime in the blood vessels. In addition to grapefruit, you can eat ripe cherries. Along with this, it is recommended to drink 7-8 glasses of water a day.

It is recommended to eat watermelon, which is not only a diuretic, but also helps to remove excess cholesterol from the body.

In order to prevent and during the treatment of atherosclerosis, sunflower oil is used, which contains a lot of unsaturated fatty acids.

In addition, people over 40 years of age suffering from atherosclerosis are advised to regularly drink raw potato juice on an empty stomach. To do this, grate a medium-sized potato tuber along with the husk on a fine grater, squeeze the juice through gauze, mix with the sediment and drink. This procedure is recommended to be repeated daily for several days. If necessary, the course can be repeated.

In addition to those drugs that are used in the treatment of cerebral atherosclerosis, some folk methods are also used. Basically, they allow you to maintain the elasticity of the walls of the arteries and slow down the formation of plaques, and also help to increase the body's resistance and, as a result, remove cholesterol from the body. All folk remedies for the treatment of atherosclerosis, listed below, are based on medicinal plants.

Hawthorn fruit juice

Mash ripe hawthorn fruits (0.5 kg), add to the resulting mass of cold water (0.5 cups), stir and heat over low heat to 40 ° C. Cool the resulting mixture and squeeze it in a juicer. This juice is recommended to be taken daily, 1 tablespoon 3 times a day before meals.

Rosehip tincture

Take ripe rose hips and crush them thoroughly, fill bottles with a mass of 0.6 and pour vodka over the contents. It is recommended to insist in a dark cool place for 2 weeks. In this case, you need to shake the bottle every day. After the tincture is ready, you should take it 20 drops per piece of sugar.

Note: This recipe can be used to make a tincture of whole rose hips. But there are slight differences when using tincture for medicinal purposes: you need to start with 5 drops, increasing the dose daily by 5 drops. When the dose reaches 100 drops, you need to gradually reduce it in the same way.

Plantain leaf tincture

Dry crushed plantain leaves (1 tablespoon) brew with boiling water (1 cup). Infuse for 10 min. drink the resulting infusion for 1 hour (daily dose).

Plantain juice

Thoroughly washed plantain leaves finely chopped, mashed and squeezed. Then mix the resulting juice with honey (1: 1) and cook for 20 minutes.

Ready infusion take 2-3 tablespoons per day. This product is recommended to be stored in a closed container in a dark, cool place.

Buckwheat flower tincture

Sowing buckwheat flowers (1 tablespoon) pour boiling water (2 cups). Infuse for 2 hours in a closed container. After the flowers are infused, strain the liquid. The resulting infusion drink 0.5 cup 3-4 times a day.

A decoction of wild strawberry leaves

Pour crushed strawberry leaves (20 g) with boiling water (1 cup) and boil for 5–10 minutes. After that, the resulting broth insist for 2 hours, and then strain through gauze.

Take a decoction daily, 1 tablespoon 3-4 times a day. Since wild strawberry leaves are a good diuretic, a large amount of cholesterol is excreted from the patient's body along with urine.

A decoction of the roots cyanosis blue

For a decoction, crushed cyanosis roots (2 tablespoons) are used, which are poured with boiling water (100 ml). Cook on low heat for water bath for 10 min. After this, the broth should be filtered.

It is recommended to take 1 tablespoon 5 times a day after meals. In this case, the last portion of the drug should be taken at bedtime.

This decoction is considered a stronger sedative than valerian (10 times stronger). Therefore, it is recommended to use it with increased excitability of the central nervous system. It also lowers blood cholesterol levels and improves the condition of the aorta by reducing lipoid deposits.

Horseradish root decoction

Take 250 g of horseradish, rinse it and dry it (but do not keep it in water). Then you should grate it on a coarse grater, pour boiled water (3 l) and put on low heat for 20 minutes. After the broth boils, it must be filtered through gauze and drunk 0.3 cups 3 times a day.

Sea kale (kelp sugar)

It is recommended to take seaweed in powder form, 0.5 teaspoon per day.

Note: the product should not be used for medicinal purposes during pregnancy, as well as for diathesis, nephritis, urticarial and chronic rhinitis.

Melissa

Melissa is considered a good remedy for vascular spasms, dizziness and tinnitus, and it also improves brain function.

As a drug against atherosclerosis, lemon balm can be used both fresh and dried. Usually it is added to tea or a decoction is prepared from it: for 200 ml of boiled water, 1 tablespoon of lemon balm. The use of lemon balm for medicinal purposes has no contraindications, so it can be taken for a long time.

Onion with garlic

These components can be used in any form (grated or whole, in the form of juice). It is recommended to take them together with honey (1:1 or 1:2). Juice should be taken 1 tablespoon before meals 3-4 times a day.

Onion syrup

There are two ways to prepare this syrup.

1. Grate one large onion on a fine grater and cover with sugar (0.5 cups). This mixture should be infused for days. It is necessary to take this syrup 1 tablespoon, 1 hour after a meal (or an hour before a meal) 3 times a day.

2. Grate one large onion and cover with granulated sugar (1 cup).

Infuse this mixture for 3-4 hours. Take the prepared syrup, you need 1 tablespoon every 3 hours.

A course of treatment lasts for 1 month. Horseradish with sour cream

Grated horseradish (1 tablespoon) mixed with sour cream (1 cup). Take the prepared mixture with meals, 1 tbsp. spoon 3-4 times a day.

Tincture from garlic

For the treatment of atherosclerosis, garlic tincture is often used, which is prepared in many ways.

1. Fill the bottle halfway with crushed garlic and fill it with vodka. It is necessary to insist for 12 days in a dark, cool place. In this case, the bottle should be shaken every day. After the tincture is ready, take 5 drops diluted in boiled water 3 times a day 15 minutes before meals.

2. Washed and peeled garlic (300

g) put in a bottle and pour alcohol. It is necessary to insist within 3 weeks. After the tincture is ready for use, you should take 20 drops every day in 0.5 cups of milk.

3. Peeled and crushed garlic (50 g) pour vodka (1 cup). It is necessary to insist within 3 days. Take this infusion should be within 3 days, 8-10 drops in a teaspoon of cold water.

4. Fill the bottle a third with finely chopped garlic, then pour alcohol or vodka and seal it tightly. It is necessary to insist in a warm (preferably sunny) place for 2 weeks. Take a ready-made infusion 1 time per day (preferably at lunchtime), starting with 2 drops. In this case, the dose should be increased by one drop every day. When the dose reaches 25 drops, it should be reduced in reverse order (up to 2 drops). After that, it is better to take a break for 2 weeks and repeat the course of treatment again.

Tincture of the roots and bark of Eleuthero coccus senticosus

Regular use of eleuthero coccus senticosus as an anti-sclerotic agent can achieve good results, since this plant lowers cholesterol levels in the blood, improves efficiency, reduces body fatigue, and improves immunity.

Eleuthero coccus has ant sclerotic properties, collected in spring during sap flow or in autumn after the leaves of plants wither. Collected Eleuther ococcus should be insisted on vodka (in a ratio of 1: 1). When the tincture darkens and acquires a specific sweet smell, it can be used for therapeutic purposes. It is necessary to take the prepared infusion 30 drops 3 times a day before meals.

In folkIn medicine, there are many ways to prepare more complex drugs. Usually, several components are used to prepare such fees. Below are a few traditional medicine recipes, the overall goal of which is to lower blood cholesterol levels.

1. Mix 1 head of garlic sowing (50 g), blood-red hawthorn flowers (25 g), and white mistletoe leaves (25 g). Pour 1 teaspoon of the mixture with boiling water (1 cup) and leave to infuse overnight.

Drink this infusion 1 glass 3 times a day.

2. Potentilla roots and leaves, dandelion roots, yarrow grass, couch grass rhizome (10 g of each component), mix 1 tablespoon of this collection with boiling water (1 cup) and leave for 1 hour.

Ready infusion must be drunk 0.75 cups before breakfast.

3. The fruits of wild strawberries, the fruits of blood-red hawthorn, the fruits of aronia chokeberry (15 g of each component) mix, 2 tbsp. l. of this collection, pour

boiled water (500 ml) and heat in a water bath for 30 minutes. Then cool the broth for 10 minutes, strain through cheesecloth and add boiled water to the original volume (500 ml).

Drink the prepared broth 0.5 cup 3-4 times a day.

4. Small periwinkle leaves, cinnamon rose hips, berries mix common raspberries, sweet clover herb, blood-red hawthorn flowers, horse chestnut flowers, nettle leaves (10 g of each component), mix, pour 1 tablespoon of this collection with boiling water (1 cup) and leave for 2 hours.

Take this infusion is necessary for 0.25 cups 3 times a day.

5. Mix horsetail herb (15 g), small periwinkle leaves (15 g), blood-red hawthorn flowers (15 g), white mistletoe grass (15 g), common yarrow grass (30 g).

Collection of these herbs (10 g) pour 1 glass of water and heat in a water bath for 15 minutes. It is necessary to cool the broth for 45 min, then strain through cheesecloth and add boiled water to it to the original volume.

The resulting decoction should be taken within1 day several times.

6. Mix common corn stigmas (10 g), common lingonberry leaves (10 g), chamomile flowers (10 g), brittle buckthorn bark (10 g), blood-red hawthorn fruits (15 g), five-lobed motherwort herb (10 g) , thallus of seaweed (10 g), fruits of aronia chokeberry (15 g), grass of a series of tripartite (10 g).

Pour this collection (10 g) with boiled water (200 ml) and heat in a water bath for 15 minutes. Then cool and strain through cheesecloth. In the resulting broth, add boiled water to the original volume (200 ml).

Drink 0.3–0.5 cup 3 times a day after meals.

7. Mix peppermint herb (10 g), leaves and fruits of cassia holly (10 g), cinnamon rosehips (15 g), birch leaves (10 g), kidney tea grass (10 g), carrot seeds (10 g) , grass cudweed marsh (10 g), eleuthero coccus senticosus root (15 g), burdock root (10 g).

Prepared and used as the previous decoction.

Parkinsonism

Tithe disease is chronic, it is caused by a violation of the metabolism of catecholamine's in the subcortical ganglia and manifests itself in the form of akinesia, tremor and muscle rigidity. The disease develops due to the impact of many causes on the subcortical ganglia. This may be a primary insufficiency of the enzymatic structures of the caudatonigral complex, drug intoxication (taking antipsychotics, reserpine, dopegyt), encephalitis, craniocerebral trauma, brain tumors.

The most common idiopathic form of the disease is Parkinson's disease and drug-induced Parkinsonism, in which there is a decrease in the content of catecholamines in the caudate nucleus and substantia nigra of the midbrain, which leads to dysfunction of the extrapyramidal system.

With the disease, a triad of symptoms is constantly observed: akinesia, rigidity and muscle tremor. The patient has a violation of gait, vegetative disorders and pain appear. The idiopathic form of the disease most often occurs after 50 years of age and begins with hand trembling, partial or general stiffness. But gradually tremor and akinesia become generalized, muscle rigidity appears with a gradual increase in tone in the limbs with repeated passive movements and jerky hypertension, a gear wheel phenomenon is observed.

When the disease changes posture and gait. Patients stoop, move in small steps. At the same time, the friendliness of the movement of the hands when walking disappears (acheirokinesis). Mimicry becomes impoverished, the face becomes like a mask, and blinking becomes rare.

Paradoxical kinesias are observed: the patient, unable to move without assistance, can easily run up the stairs, ski and dance. In some cases, propulsion is observed: slow movement is suddenly replaced by a fast run. The patient runs until he encounters an obstacle or falls. There is also an increase in skin greasiness (hyper salivation) and impaired urination. But at the same time, muscle strength remains normal, the reflex and sensory spheres do not suffer. In severe cases or in the late stage of the disease, the patient is almost completely immobilized and cannot get out of bed even with outside help.

Treatment

With drug-induced Parkinsonism, the dose of drugs used is reduced or neutralizers are administered. In other cases, use medopar-125 and nakom. Along with this, the doctor also prescribes central anticholinergics: midantan, parlodel and amitriptyline. But, in addition to drug therapy, massage and physiotherapy exercises are no less important. The patient must remember that the bed is the main enemy of the parkinsonian, and in this regard, it is necessary to constantly be as active as possible. The movement contains a very effective treatment and even getting rid of the disease.

In addition to the fact that physical exercises have a beneficial effect on the patient's condition, certain nutrition plays a positive role in the treatment of this disease. Therefore, to improve the condition of a patient with Parkinsonism, doctors recommend eating more fruits and vegetables, which, as you know, contain many useful minerals and vitamins, as well as some berries (cherries, sweet cherries, barberries).Vegetables and fruits are best consumed raw, as processing leads to the destruction of vitamins. Salads from vegetables and fruits are very useful.

Polyneuropathies

Polyneuropathy or polyneuritis is a simultaneous lesion of many peripheral nerves, which manifests itself in symmetrical flaccid paralysis and sensory disturbances, mainly in the distal extremities. In some cases, this is a lesion of the cranial nerves.

The disease can develop as a result of intoxication (poisoning with alcohol, gasoline, lead, arsenic, sulfonamides), Para infectious and allergic complications of diphtheria, pneumonia and par otitis, dys metabolic disorders (diabetes mellitus, uremia, porphyria), malnutrition (deficiency of vitamins B1, B12), systemic diseases (per arteritis), malignant tumors.

The disease occurs at any age, but people of young and middle age are more often ill. With polyneuropathies, muscle weakness, atrophy, paresthesia, pain, hyperesthesia or anesthesia, decreased or loss of reflexes are observed. These disorders are most pronounced in the distal extremities and rarely extend to the body.

The course of the disease is caused by a sensitivity disorder (most often vibrational). Due to paralysis of the feet, step page (cock's gait) occurs, and in severe cases, tetraplegia is recorded. Muscles and nerve trunks are painful on palpation, trophic disorders occur (dryness and cyanosis of the skin, damage to the nails).

Treatment

Since this disease is characterized by a deficiency of B vitamins, this moment is taken into account in the treatment.

That is why the following foods containing these vitamins are included in the diet of patients with polyneuritis: potatoes, cabbage, carrots, apples, tomatoes, lettuce, pears, turnips, spinach, nuts, and oats.

Multiple sclerosis

This is a remitting disease of the nervous system, which is caused by the occurrence of demyelination foci scattered throughout the brain and spinal cord (Fig. 1).

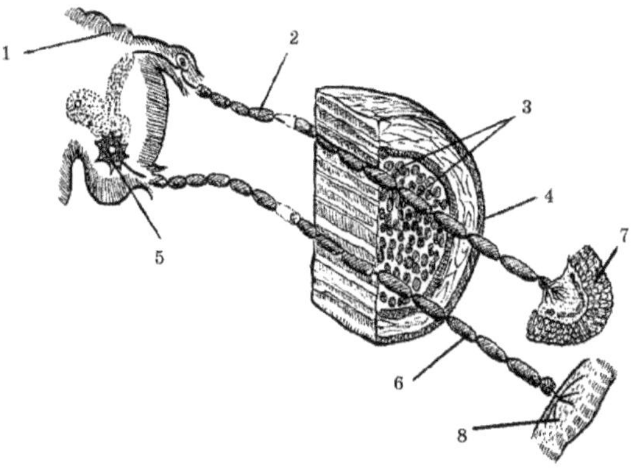

Rice. 1. The structure of the nerve: 1 - spinal cord; 2 - sensitive neuron; 3 - bundles of nerve fibers; 4 - nerve

sheath; 5 - motor neuron; 6 - myelin sheath; 7 - skin; 8 - muscle

Demyelination process affects mainly the white matter of the central nervous system. The damaged area of the neuron may also undergo demyelination. Following the breakdown of myelin, axons are also damaged (Fig. 2), followed by the development of a characteristic glial plaque.

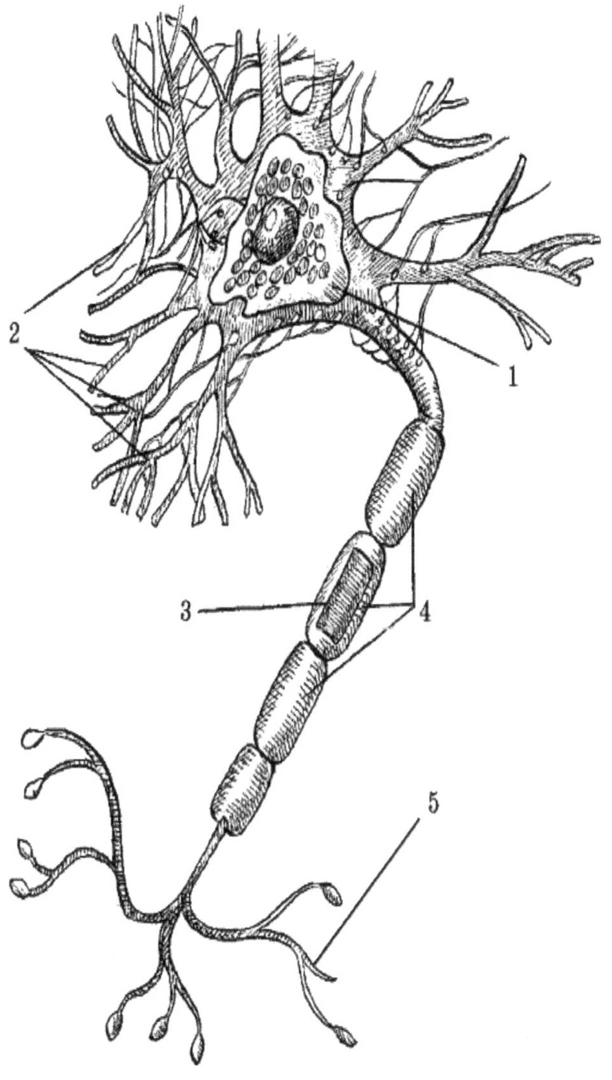

Rice. 2. Structure of a neuron: 1 -

body; 2 - dendrite; 3 - myelin sheath; 4 - axons; 5 - the end of the axon

The disease occurs at a young age (children and the elderly are extremely rarely affected). The first symptoms are transient. These are motor, sensory (usually paresthesia) or visual disturbances. More often than others, the pyramidal and cerebellar systems and the optic nerves are affected with age. In the advanced stage of the disease, a rough tremor of the limbs is usually observed, less often of the head (trembling is detected during active movement), but the disease can also be static.

Multiple sclerosis is characterized by a remitting course: exacerbations are replaced by significant improvements, all or some signs of the disease often disappear completely. The duration of remissions is different: from several days to several years.

Treatment

At the beginning and during the exacerbation of the disease, glucocorticoid hormones or ACTH, immune suppressors and immune modulators are used. During periods of remission, a decisive role is played by massage, the prevention of undercurrent infections (urological sepsis, pneumonia).

Regarding nutrition in this disease, it should be noted that the use of dairy products, especially cream and sour milk, is very useful for patients. They can be consumed daily, 1 glass per day, if desired - more. Milk porridges are also useful.

Migraine

This is a disease, the consequence of which is the expansion of the blood vessels of the brain. It has already been established that a simple headache is very different from migraine. The difference lies in the following: unlike migraine, a headache begins gradually, that is, the strength of pain does not increase immediately. Migraine is a throbbing headache. Most often, it proceeds paroxysmal and lasts approximately 12–18 hours. Specialists distinguish 2 types of migraine:

– classical, when an attack is preceded by a general deterioration in a person's condition, there is a feeling of flickering light in the eyes or a temporary loss of vision; normal, without any harbingers of an attack.

As a rule, migraines appear at regular intervals. In a month, attacks can be repeated from 2 to 4 times. According to scientific observations, they are caused by stressful situations when a person is in a state of the highest tension. In addition, the reason for the appearance migraine attacks is the use of certain foods (chocolate, caffeinated food, chicken liver, citrus fruits, sausage, aged cheeses). Attacks can be accelerated by the use of alcoholic beverages, as well as general fatigue of the body, its hypothermia, sudden changes in temperature.

The word "migraine" means not just a severe headache, but a specific diagnosis, which means pain that usually starts on one side of the head, but from attack to attack, pain can move from one side to the other. Often the pain is accompanied by nausea, as well as an exacerbation of sensitivity to light and sounds.

A migraine attack is often accompanied by other symptoms: a person experiences numbness of the skin of the face, chills, his limbs become cold. This is also accompanied by vomiting, diarrhea, dizziness, frequent urination, decreased attention, extreme susceptibility to light or noise, and in the initial phase - difficulty in speech and impaired muscle control. It is not surprising that after the most acute phase of the attack has passed, it seems to the person that he is completely exhausted mentally and physically.

About 11% of the population suffers from migraine, and about 10% of them have classic-type migraine, when the headache is preceded by a phase of perceptual disturbance called an aura. It lasts 10-30 minutes, and during this time, flies flash before the eyes of a person or they are covered with a veil, and bright flashes appear. In addition, hearing and speech deteriorate, the sense of balance is disturbed.

This is because the brain does not receive enough blood as a result of the sudden narrowing of the major cerebral arteries. The cause of this phenomenon has not yet been fully understood, but experts are investigating the substance serotonin, since it has been found that immediately after the aura stage, its level in the brain rises, and that it is able to cause vasoconstriction.

Headache due to its occurrence

can be divided into 3 main categories:

– arising from muscle tension;

– Caused by some latent disease in the body; vascular, which, in fact, is called migraine.

Migraine is the second most common type headache after headache associated with mental exertion and indirect tension of the muscles of the head and neck. These two types of headaches often coexist and migraine patients can easily tell them apart. The main difference is that a tension-type headache comes on and develops gradually, while a migraine attack occurs suddenly and in the presence of other symptoms.

According to statistics, in 90% of the population, the cause of a headache is quite simple: excessive or too long muscle tension, for example, from an uncomfortable posture. Vascular headache, or migraine, as well as that resulting from an underlying illness, are much less common.

Usually, the symptoms of headaches of muscle origin resemble those that arise due to other causes, but in general, signs that characterize muscle headaches can be distinguished:

– Moderation of pain, while it itself is not sharp and throbbing, but steady and dull. It is often compared to squeezing the head in a vise;

– pain duration from 30 minutes to several days;

– the occurrence of pain equally on both sides of the head, as well as pain in the muscles of the shoulders and neck or their numbness;

– no increase in headache with continued normal

– physical activity;

– loss of appetite, but no nausea or

vomiting;

– emotional stress or feeling depressed;

– Absence of other diseases or any abnormal conditions.

There is also a mixed headache, in which there are signs of both vascular pain and that caused by muscle tension. Some experts believe that these two types of headaches have not so little similarity as previously thought.

With a headache caused by muscle tension, it is not difficult to determine its cause. This may be a quarrel with a loved one, and a conflict at work, as well as troubles or problems that have arisen, driving a car for too long.

Vascular headache - followed by prevalence. It depends on the level of blood pressure and manifests itself in pain sensations of varying degrees, both at elevated and at its reduced level. Both disorders respond poorly to therapeutic treatment. In both cases, the pain is localized in the occipital region of the head and is accompanied by general malaise.

Another type of headache is a relatively rare focal headache, which is rightfully considered by neurologists to be the most painful of those that a person can experience. The so-called cluster headache will be discussed below.

The emotional state of a person plays a very important role in the appearance of a headache. Most often, headaches are psychogenic in nature, that is, they are caused by some special emotional state. In this case, the effect of real pain occurs.

Pain-producing emotions are intense or persistent stress, anxiety, or anger. The states experienced as a result of the occurrence of these emotions lead to a prolonged contraction of the muscles of the face, scalp, shoulders or neck, and therefore to a muscle tension headache, as well as to vasodilation in these areas, which causes a vascular headache.

Unpleasant emotions that negatively affect the body and headache are interrelated: the former provoke pain, which, in turn, contribute to the emergence of an unfavorable emotional state.

Moreover, the stronger and more painful the pain, the greater the fear of it. Occurrence and, as a result, more likely that a headache will actually occur.

Migraine in women

Migraine is a disease predominantly of women. According to statistics, the female half of the population suffers from this disease three times more often than the male. In addition, migraine attacks can intensify and become more frequent against the background of hormonal changes associated with the age and physiological characteristics of the female body, as well as various gynecological diseases.

Another female problem is menopause, when significant changes occur in the body. As a rule, migraine progresses with its onset. Menopause is a physiological process associated with the cessation of a woman's reproductive function. This period is also characterized by hormonal changes in the body and means a decrease in the production of female hormones. Because of this, a number of pathological processes occur in a woman's body: the appearance of episodic rises in blood pressure, osteoporosis - rarefaction of the bone structure, exacerbation of chronic and psychosomatic diseases.

Most often, this decline takes place abruptly, as a result of which such unpleasant sensations as hot flashes arise. In addition, chronic diseases can worsen. Migraines often get worse. And if earlier it could be eliminated with the help of various means - from analgesics to tying the head with a towel, now it becomes simply uncontrollable. Headache acquires a diffuse character, spreads to neighboring areas.

Characteristic of menopausal migraine is that analgesics lose their effectiveness. Removing a headache becomes quite a challenge. The use of hormonal drugs that weaken the pathological course of menopause can reduce the frequency and intensity of migraine attacks.

At this time, you should constantly consult with an endocrinologist, who will prescribe the most suitable drugs as replacement therapy, and also register with a neurologist. It will help in the prevention and elimination of seizures. It is also recommended to avoid psych traumatic situations, factors that provoke a migraine attack.

You should not self-medicate, as the frequent use of conventional analgesics is not safe for health and can contribute to an even greater frequency of attacks and their severity. Better seek help from a qualified medical specialist.

Migraine has also been associated with premenstrual syndrome (PMS). Its presence is associated with a number of individual characteristics of a woman. The premenstrual period lasts from the 14th to the 28th day of the cycle, at which time mild headaches occur. They are usually referred to as tension headaches or as a combination of migraine and tension headache. Although their strength and intensity are small, they cause trouble in combination with the whole complex of symptoms of premenstrual syndrome. For example, they include a range of emotional, physical and behavioral disorders.

Also, to other features of the female body, you can add increased pain sensitivity, a hereditary factor, inflammatory gynecological diseases, hypothalamic syndrome, and neuroendocrine disorders. In the presence of the latter, migraine has the most pronounced attacks? PMS can also be affected by prolonged stress, pregnancy and childbirth.

In medical practice, for the treatment of severe PMS, antidepressants are used, which are also drugs for the prevention of migraine. Oral contraceptives are often prescribed to reduce PMS. But they do not affect the course of migraine, and sometimes even increase it. Conventional analgesics used to relieve PMS are ineffective for migraine attacks. Important here is the observance of the regime of work and rest, sleep and wakefulness, reduction of psycho-emotional stress, normal nutrition.

Male migraine

The course of migraine in a strong half of humanity has its own characteristics. Here, the role of hormonal changes is excluded, since the physiological cyclist in men is much less pronounced than in women. External factors are of the greatest importance. For example, it is known that men are more prone to stress. In addition, they are more likely than women to occupy high positions that require great responsibility and employment, which in turn leads to emotional overload.

Also, men are more prone to bad habits than women and pay less attention to their health. Migraine attacks in them occur less frequently than in the female half of the population, but proceed more intensively. Often the pain is somewhat different in symptoms from migraine. It begins, as a rule, in the middle of the night, with a pain of blurry localization. The attack comes on suddenly and can last for a few seconds, and then passes, resuming after a while.

In this case, you may need other treatment and advice from an experienced specialist. According to statistics, nocturnal migraine occurs in 20% of patients. The hereditary factor plays a big role here. If one of the patient's relatives suffered from nocturnal migraine, most likely the migraine will occur at the same time of day.

From a psychological point of view, nocturnal migraine can be explained as follows. Patients suffering from nocturnal migraine have a number of traumatic situations in their subconscious that have happened to them in the past. During the period of wakefulness, consciousness displaces them, and a person may not remember them, but during sleep, psychodramas are realized and actualized. This property of the psyche is often used by psychoanalysts in the treatment of certain diseases, including migraine. A person, being in a state of hypnosis, talks aloud about his internal conflicts, as if re-experiencing a traumatic situation. Thus, he gets rid of fears, fears, doubts and other negative emotions inherent in the subconscious, thereby losing the colossal stress that is the cause of the disease.

Treatment

As noted by many experts, migraine is in most cases a food reaction to certain foods. In this case, the reaction of the body to these stimuli occurs when the so-called histamines are formed in the tissues, which cause the expansion of blood vessels. Usually a person suffering from frequent migraine attacks knows which foods are contraindicated for him. In addition, foods containing B vitamins are known to help prevent migraines. Vitamins of this group (riboflavin and pyridoxine) contribute to the narrowing of blood vessels by increasing the production of serotonin in the brain, as well as reducing the number and frequency of migraine attacks.

In the treatment of migraine, the substances contained in the following products are useful:

– flax seeds, marinefish;

– corn, soybean and cottonseed oils;

– Nuts, cumin, almonds, avocado, olive oil.

If the migraine does not recede, traditional medicine advises using the following methods: Break a raw egg into a glass and pour boiled milk over it. Then stir very quickly and drink immediately. This procedure must be repeated for several days;

– wrap the sauerkraut in a cloth and put it on your ears, and then tightly tie a towel around your head;

– Moisten a cotton swab with beet or onion juice and put it in the ear.

In order to prevent migraine it is necessary:

– carefully eat foods, that is, exclude from the diet those that can provoke the appearance of headaches;

– lead a healthy lifestyle and exercise regularly;

– do not overload your body with various intellectual loads;

– Limit external stimuli that can trigger a migraine (radio, television, etc.).

As mentioned above, migraine attacks can provoke the use of certain products, which include certain components that are the cause of the headache. These include the following substances:

– aspartame (sweetener);

– phenethylamine (found in chocolate);

– atrazine (food coloring, a flavor enhancer used in the

manufacture of certain semi-finished products);

– tyramine (found in sausages, beef and chicken liver, cheese, soy sauce, salted fish);

– Glutamate (found in wines, champagne, cocoa and chocolate).

All these products in the presence of a predisposition to migraine attacks are recommended to be excluded from the diet.

Myopathy

It belongs to a group of diseases characterized by progressive muscular dystrophy. Myopathy is a chronic pathology of the neuromuscular apparatus. In addition, it is hereditary. The occurrence of myopathy is also due to complications of various kinds: infectious diseases, injuries, colds, etc. There is an assumption that the cause of the disease is a pathological violation of the metabolic processes of cyclic nucleotides, which are universal regulators of cyclic metabolism responsible for the implementation of genetic information.

It has been established that women are carriers of myopathy, but only men suffer from it. This picture is observed in 50% of cases.

In patients with myopathy, cardinal disorders of the nervous system are not observed, although there is a decrease in the cells of the anterior roots of the spinal cord. The most significant pathological changes occur in the striated muscles: they become thin, and most of their fibers are replaced by connective tissue and fat. At the same time, characteristic changes in muscle fibers are observed: they are randomly intertwined with healthy fibers. Muscle fibers split lengthwise, forming vacuoles.

During the course of the disease,

there is a gradual replacement of muscles with adipose or connective tissue. This leads to progressive (partial or complete) muscle atrophy. During the course of the disease, patients noticeably lose weight, and they also experience paresis.

The process of atrophy is rather slow, muscle groups are affected unevenly, so patients with myopathy are able not only to serve themselves, but also continue to be efficient. At the same time, they retain sensitivity in the limbs, and motor functions (coordination of movements) are also not disturbed.

In the final stage of the disease, the patient has pathological disorders of the cardiovascular activity, while there are changes in body temperature and pulse, there is an increase in sweating, and respiratory activity worsens.

Treatment

Usually, during the treatment of myopathy, doctors prescribe a course of vitamins, in addition, it is recommended to do a light massage and physiotherapy exercises. Since patients with myopathy are often prone to infectious and catarrhal diseases, they must be protected. In addition, for such people it is advised to provide a quiet, calm environment in the house.

As medicines, it is recommended to include in the diet more fruits and vegetables (preferably daily), containing a wide range of vitamins. In addition, do not forget about the recipes of traditional medicine, which are not rejected by doctors either.

Patients with myopathy are recommended to give infusions of medicinal herbs. In this case, it is appropriate to use such herbs as aralia, Siberian hogweed, common valerian, three-leaf watch.

Aralia Manchurian tincture

It must be taken 15-20 drops with cooled boiled water 1-2 times a day.

Siberian hogweed infusion

Pour dry hogweed herb (3 teaspoons) with 2 cups of cold boiled water and infuse for 2 hours. After that, strain the infusion through gauze.

Prepared infusion (preferably cold) should be taken 0.25 cup 4 times a day before meals.

Valerian officinalis

This plant is widely known as it has a number of medicinal qualities. In the treatment of myopathy, it is appropriate to use valerian, since it helps to reduce reflex excitability and relieves muscle spasms.

1. Dry rhizomes and roots of valerian (1 tablespoon) insist for 12 hours in a closed glass of cooled boiled water. Take this infusion should be 1 tablespoon 3-4 times a day before

meals.

2. Rhizomes and roots of valerian insist on vodka or 70% alcohol in a ratio of 1: 5 for 1 week. After that, strain the tincture through cheesecloth. Take this remedy should be 15-20 drops 3-4 times a day.

Keep this tincture in a dry place. Cool place.

3. Valerian root powder is recommended to take 1 g 3 times a day.

Three-leaf watch

1. Watch leaves (5 g) insist in 1 cup of boiled water, then strain. Take this infusion should be 0.25 cups 4 times a day before meals.

2. Powders from the leaves of the watch should be taken 1 g 2 times a day 30 minutes before meals.

3. Leaves of the watch (0.5 teaspoon) insist in cold water for 8

hours. Take the prepared infusion should be 0.5 cup 2-4 times a day 30 minutes before meals.

In addition to the above recipes of traditional medicine, in the treatment of myopathy, it is recommended to eat cherries, which improve the patient's appetite and are considered a means of calming the nerves.

Neuralgia

This is a disease of the nervous system, characterized by acute, burning, aching or dull pain along the nerve of a specific organ.

Such pains usually begin paroxysmal, sometimes the disease is accompanied by reddening of the skin, sweating, even muscle twitching.

The causes of this disease can be different: pathological changes in the nerve plexuses, as well as processes that develop in nearby organs and tissues due to injuries, infections, even severe hypothermia. There are several types of neuralgia. The allocation of these varieties is due to the localization of neuralgic pains.

Occipital neuralgia often occurs during hard work; in women, such pain may appear during PMS.

Trigeminal neuralgia is accompanied not only by severe pain, but also by twitching of the muscles of the face, salivation or lacrimation. According to experts, the causes of these pains can be diseases of the nasal cavity and teeth, and in women - pathological disorders in the genital area.

Neuralgia of the intercostal nerves is usually accompanied by pain in the spine, namely from the side along the line from the armpit down and in front, near the sternum.

Sciatic nerve neuralgia, or sciatica,

is a disease in which the patient feels pain in the sciatic nerve and its branches. Most often, the causes of this kind of pain are infections (flu, syphilis, malaria, tuberculosis), as well as alcohol poisoning, various kinds of injuries, hypothermia, severe overwork.

With neuralgia of the sciatic nerve, pain is characteristic in the lower back and in the leg along the sciatic nerve and its branches: lower leg, heel, back of the thigh, outer surface of the foot. If the patient at the same time unbends the limb, a sharp pain is felt in the area of \u200b\u200bthe diseased nerve, sensations of numbness of the skin, coldness of the legs may appear. The muscles of the diseased limb lose their tone and become flabby.

Treatment

Similar neuralgias are usually treated with rest as w ell as sedatives. In addition, an effective way to eliminate such pains is the use of ammonia and camphor, which are moistened with a handkerchief and slowly inhaled.

In addition to the above-mentioned remedies, traditional medicine recipes are widely used in the treatment of neuralgic pain.

Decoction of common harmala

Herb harmala vulgaris (1 teaspoon) boil in 1 glass of water and infuse for 2 hours. Then you need to strain the infusion through gauze.

Take this remedy should be 1 tablespoon 3-4 times a day.

Highlander tincture serpentine

It can be prepared in two ways.

– 1 teaspoon of fresh rhizomes of this plant pour 1.5 cups of water and boil for 10 minutes. After this, the broth must be insisted for 2 hours, then strain. Take 0.5 cup 3 times a day;

– Pour 2 teaspoons of dry leaves of the plant with boiled water (1 cup) and infuse for 1 hour. Then strain the infusion. It is necessary to take this tincture in 0.25 cups 4 times a day before meals.

Tincture of sweet clover

2 tsp Plants pour 2 cups of chilled boiled water and insist in a closed vessel. Take this infusion should be 0.5 cup 2-3 times a day.

John's wort tincture

It can also be prepared in two ways:

– Dry herb St. John's wort (10 g) pour 1 cup of boiled water and leave for a short time. Prepared infusion take 1 tablespoon 2-4 times a day after meals;

– Dry grass of the plant (15–20 g) insist on alcohol or vodka (0.5 l). Take an infusion of 30 drops with water 3 times a day after meals.

Infusion of snakehead Moldavian

Infuse the dry herb of this plant (1 tablespoon), pour boiling water (1 cup) for 10-15 minutes. Then you need to strain the infusion and cool. Take the prepared remedy 1 tablespoon 3-4 times a day 15 minutes before meals.

Infusion of willow bark

Dry willow bark (1 teaspoon) insist in cooled boiled water (2 cups) for 4 hours. The prepared infusion should be taken 0.5 cup 2-4 times a day before meals.

Neuro rheumatism

This is a pathological lesion of the nervous system of a rheumatic nature. This disease affects not only the cardiovascular system, but also the joints. In this case, the peripheral parts of the nervous system, as well as the central nervous system, are often affected. Tithe disease can be caused by complex forms of pathologies, such as encephalitis or meningitis.

Children often suffer from neuro rheumatism. The disease occurs in them usually after they have had a sore throat. Wherein the prodromal period lasts approximately 2–2.5 weeks. A sick child becomes lethargic, irritable for no reason, often cries.

Characteristic is the change in handwriting, which looks unstable, jumping. A sick child blinks frequently, and twitching of all facial muscles is possible.

If all of the above symptoms are observed in a child, then it is urgent to contact a specialist who will establish the cause of the disease after examining the heart and joints, where pathological manifestations of the disease are easily detected. You may need a blood test, because pathology is sometimes found there too.

Treatment

Treatment of this disease is carried out in a hospital under the supervision of a physician. Usually patients are prescribed a course of antibiotics and hormones. Massage sessions and exercise therapy are also available. After treatment, the child should be under the supervision of a rheumatologist and a neurologist for some time. In addition, vitamins are prescribed to restore strength, and for prevention, it is advised to take bacilli.

Doctors advise eating the following foods: carrots, cabbage, potatoes, tomatoes, watermelon, beets, and cucumbers. Contraindications include the use of spicy foods (garlic, onions, etc.), as well as the addition of spicy seasonings to food.

In addition to the main medicines, it is recommended to establish a certain diet; the diet should include not only fruits and vegetables, but also some herbal infusions used in traditional medicine.

European hoof infusion

It can be prepared in two ways:

– Rhizomes of the plant (2 g) pour 1 glass of water and infuse for 2-3 hours, then strain the infusion. Take the prepared infusion 1 tablespoon 2 times a day;

– Plant leaves (1 g) pour 1 glass of cooled boiled water and infuse for 2-3 hours, then strain. Take the prepared infusion should be 1 tablespoon 2 times a day.

Common ragwort infusion

Infuse dry ragwort herb (1 teaspoon) by pouring 2 cups of boiled water for 1 hour. After that, the infusion must be cooled. Take 1 tablespoon 2-3 times a day.

Infusion of flax seed

Boil flax seeds (2 teaspoons) in 1.5 cups of water and leave for 10 minutes. Then you need to shake this infusion in a bottle for 5 minutes and strain through cheesecloth. It is necessary to take this remedy for 0.5 cups on an empty stomach.

Lemon

Since lemon is an effective pain reliever, doctors recommend eating it as a preventive measure, in particular, lemon juice is effective. You can add it to tea or water, and also use it in its pure form.

Lemongrass

With this disease, it is recommended to use an aqueous infusion of lemongrass leaves or bark, since they are good vitamin remedies.

Syringomyelia

The name of this disease in Greek means “a cavity in the spinal cord", therefore, it is a chronic form of pathology of the nervous system, in which the spinal cord is affected. In this case, the lesion occurs even during the period of intrauterine development of the embryo. In the spinal cord, cavities are formed, connected by the central canal of the nervous system.

The causes of this disease are not fully known, but there is still an assumption that heredity affects the development of syringe mycelia.

During path anatomical studies, it was found that in patients with syringe mycelia, a transverse incision revealed cavities in the cervicothoracic spinal cord, in the lateral ventricles of the brain, as well as in the medulla oblongata, as well as overgrown glial tissue.

This disease can capture not only the spinal cord, but also blood vessels and connective tissue. Other foci of pathology formation are also possible.

Most cases of syringomyelia occur in men under the age of 30. Most often this is associated with heavy physical labor (although manifestations of this disease are also possible in childhood). According to experts, the main factors that can provoke the onset and development of the disease are, first of all, a sharp drop in temperature, various kinds of injuries and hard overwork.

One of the main symptoms of this disease is the loss of sensitivity of the skin. So, for example, patients feel pain and cannot even determine whether an object is cold or hot. That is why people with syringomyelia often get painless burns. As a rule, there is a mobile localization of skin sensitivity disorders, but most often this pathology manifests itself in such areas of the skin where the cervical and thoracic nerves, as well as the lumbosacral nerves, pass. In most patients with syringomyelia, the zone of sensitivity of the trigeminal nerve is disturbed, more often in the outer zone of its innervation.

And yet patients are able to feel pain, but only in other areas, and it is this circumstance that makes them see a doctor, because they suffer first from short, and later from periodic and constant pain in the cervical or scapular region.

In addition to the fact that with syringomyelia the sensitivity of the skin is disturbed, this disease is also characterized by disorders of the musculoskeletal system. At the same time, there are minor paresis, as well as impaired reflexes. For example, patients cannot hold objects in their hands, as either atrophy of the limbs (and even partial atrophy of the tongue) or loss of tendon reflexes occurs.

In addition to the above characteristic signs of this disease, it should be mentioned that in patients with syringomyelia there is dystrophy of the bones of the skeleton, as well as curvature of the spine (kyphosis, scoliosis, and kyphoscoliosis).

With syringomyelia, painless swelling, cracks appear on the patient's skin, which heal for a very long time.

In general, syringomyelia progresses rather slowly, so patients are able to maintain working capacity for a long time.

Treatment

The course of treatment of patients with syringomyelia includes mainly amino acid preparations and protein hydrolysates, which contribute to one degree or another to restore the sensitivity of the skin. In addition, vitamin therapy is a highly effective way to treat syringomyelia. Not excluded therapeutic massage and exercise therapy, as well as spa treatment.

In general, in the treatment of syringomyelia, the most important thing is the correct implementation of preventive measures, as well as taking care of the patient and his professional orientation and ability to work.

In addition to the above recommendations for the treatment of patients with syringomyelia, proper nutrition is very important, which is set individually for each patient. First of all, the patient needs to eat those foods that include a wide range of vitamins, in particular group B (carrots, cabbage, potatoes, beets, spinach, cherries, etc.), as well as vitamin A. In addition, it is useful for such patients eating sour-milk and bakery products, since they contribute to recovery after an illness.

In folk medicine, recipes for infusions and decoctions are used, which allow to increase the sensitivity of the skin and improve the general condition of patients with syringomyelia. First of all, in the treatment of this disease, tinctures of such plants as chestnut, medicinal gooseberry, Dahurian black cohosh, clover, etc. are used. Here are the recipes for preparing these infusions.

1. **Capers are prickly.** Boil the bark of dried caper roots (2 teaspoons) for 10-15 minutes, pour 1 cup of boiling water, leave for 30 minutes, then strain. Take the prepared infusion 1 tablespoon 3-4 times a day.

2. **Chestnut.** Infuse 1 teaspoon of chestnut bark for 8 hours, pour 2 cups of cooled boiled water, then strain. Prepared infusion take 0.25 cup 4 times a day before meals.

3. **Clover hybrid.** This plant allows you to remove aches in the affected areas of the patient's body:

– 3 teaspoons of herb clover hybrid insist 2 hours, pour 1 glass of boiling water. Prepared infusion take 1 tablespoon 4 times a day;

– Pour boiling water over 2-3

tablespoons of clover grass, wrap in gauze. Apply compresses to inflamed areas of the skin and sore spots.

4. **Black cohosh Dahurian.**1 part of rhizomes and roots of black cohosh insist 5 days in 5 parts of 70% alcohol. Prepared infusion take 20-30 drops with boiled water 2-3 times a day.

5. Hypertension

The word "hypertension" ("hypertension") from the Latin language is translated as "increased pressure, increased tone." This is an increase in blood pressure. High blood pressure is not always a sign of illness, in some conditions the pressure rises even in healthy people: after jogging behind a bus, visiting a steam room, any conflict, not only pressure will increase, but also respiratory rate, pulse, skin temperature, and other characteristics will change. In a healthy person, they quickly return to normal.

In some cases, hypertension can be caused by a disease of internal organs (for example, kidneys). In this case, it is a symptom of another disease.

Actually hypertension is a condition, the main symptom of which is an increase in blood pressure, not caused by organic diseases. The basis of this disease is a gradual, but significant increase in the tension of the walls of all small arteries, as a result of which their lumen decreases and the passage of blood through the vessels becomes more difficult. That is why the pressure of blood on the walls of blood vessels increases.

The prevalence of hypertension

Hypertension ranks first in prevalence among non-communicable diseases. It is no coincidence that a huge number of studies in different countries of the world are devoted to the epidemiology of this disease, including a number of programs where hundreds of thousands of people belonging to different sex, age, occupational, ethnic and other groups of the population are examined and observed by the same methods in different cities. True, with such studies it can be difficult to establish the causes of increased blood pressure.

The epidemiological material showed that the efforts of physicians should be directed to the prevention of this disease, the formation of a healthy lifestyle, and if the disease has already occurred, to delay its progression, prevent complications (cerebral strokes, myocardial infarction, kidney disease, etc.).

Scientists have proposed formulas for calculating blood pressure according to age: systolic (maximum) pressure = 102 + (0.6 x age), diastolic (minimum) pressure = 63 + (0.4 x age). For example, a person is 25 years old. In this case, his blood pressure should not be higher than 117/73 mm Hg. Art.

There are stages in a person's life when the risk of hypertension increases. First of all, these are periods when the function of the endocrine apparatus changes, the hormonal balance in the body is disturbed.

Hormonal disorders often occur during menopause, when the activity of the gonads fades away, especially if it happens rather quickly, in the form of a jump. In some men and women in the menopause, there is an instability of pressure, a tendency to rise. Subsequently, the pressure may return to normal. Menopause contributes to the more frequent occurrence of neuroses and the weakening of the regulatory systems of the body due to the restructuring of metabolic processes.

During puberty - the same stage in hormonal balance - autonomic nervous mechanisms are especially labile, the relationship between the nervous and endocrine regulation of blood pressure is easily disrupted and, as a result, hypertension can develop.

The current generation develops hypertension 15–20 years earlier than the previous one. The disease seems to start in early childhood and may be related to the information boom that children are experiencing, with a huge amount of knowledge that they have to learn in the course of the educational process. An important role is also played by hereditary background. In families where one or both parents suffer from hypertension, children are 2.5 times more likely to develop this disease than children of healthy parents.

Researchers note that both systolic and diastolic blood pressure increase with age, especially in young men. The incidence of arterial hypertension in urban and rural areas in recent years differs insignificantly.

Among the causes of the disease, the main one is considered a genetic predisposition. Hypertension is often a family disease. Contribute to the emergence and development of the disease severe and frequent stress, psychophysical overload. Hypertension is extremely difficult to tolerate if it is accompanied by obesity. The use of salty and spicy foods and alcohol provokes seizures.

At the initial stage of the disease, under the influence of stress and repetitive negative emotions, the balance of the nervous and endocrine mechanisms responsible for the regulation of blood circulation is disturbed. At the same time, the activity of the sympathetic department of the nervous system and the production of adrenaline by the body increase. As a result, the strength and frequency of heart contractions increase, the maximum pressure and blood supply to tissues increase.

Baroreceptors located in the walls of the aorta and the most important arteries are called upon to restore the disturbed balance. They signal the actual blood pressure to the vasomotor centers. Signals will be received until substances such as bradykinin are produced, causing vasodilation and a decrease in pressure. During this period, renal blood flow may decrease, which will lead to the release of the enzyme renin by the kidneys, which indirectly contributes to an increase in blood pressure: it stimulates the production of the hormone aldosterone by the adrenal glands, which regulates water-salt metabolism in the body.

Under the action of aldosterone, the excretion of sodium and water in the urine decreases, that is, the volume of circulating blood increases, and the sodium content in the cells of the body, including the smooth muscles of the arterial vessels, also increases.

Following sodium, water is attracted to the cells, they swell, and there is a decrease in the lumen of the vessels, which leads to an increase in pressure. A quarter of patients with hypertension consume an excess amount of table salt - sodium chloride.

In the initial stage of hypertension, self-defense mechanisms are activated: after the release of renin, the kidneys begin to produce prostaglandins, which contribute to vasodilation. As a result, the pressure returns to normal.

If irritating factors act constantly, the body's compensatory capabilities are exhausted and the disease stabilizes. Under the influence of a prolonged increase in blood pressure, baroreceptors are tuned to a high level of pressure, as to the norm.

Stojko rises tone of a huge network of arterioles impaired renal blood flow, exchange of sodium and other substances, changes in work endocrine glands. Under such conditions, answer on the action epinephrine renin or adrenaline pressure rises even more. It can be normalized only by active medical intervention. According to the latest recommendations World organizations health care, a blood pressure of 140/90 mm Hg is considered normal. Art. And below. Pressure 160/95 mm Hg. Art. Is elevated. Persons under 40 years of age whose blood pressure fluctuates within these limits are considered prone to hypertension and should be observed by a doctor.

Blood pressure in children is lower than in adults. Regardless of the age of the child, it should not exceed 130/80 mm Hg. Art. Scientists noted that high blood pressure in schoolchildren aged 12–13 after 5 years persists only in 40% of cases.

The pressure changes throughout the day. Most often, the minimum indicators occur at night, during sleep, between 11 pm and 3 am. The highest indicators occur at the end of the day, when fatigue accumulates, between 5 pm and 8 pm. experienced, etc.

Not everyone tolerates high blood pressure painfully. Sometimes people can live with hypertension for many years without much deterioration in well-being, without losing their ability to work. This is especially true of the initial stage of the disease.

A typical symptom of hypertension is headache, heaviness in the back of the head, which sometimes appears already in the morning, often accompanied by flashing before the eyes, dizziness, and sometimes nausea. In some cases, nosebleeds occur, leading to relief of the condition. It is not always the case that the higher the pressure, the worse the headache. Headaches are more painful with a sharp change in pressure.

Hypertonic disease usually

develops gradually. Pressure rises are short-lived. In some cases, there are sleep disturbances, increased irritability, headaches, occasionally palpitations and discomfort in the heart. Then there are more complaints, efficiency decreases, pressure rises more often. An electrocardiogram shows left ventricular overload.

Hypertensive disease proceeds unevenly. It is characterized by periods of exacerbations, in severe cases - crises. Sometimes it can stabilize for a while. In rare cases, the pressure steadily returns to normal without any complications.

The modern method of measuring pressure does not provide information about all areas of blood circulation. Hypertension in any organ is possible with normal pressure in the brachial artery.

In recent years, an idea has appeared about target organs that suffer more than others from a violation of pressure: these are blood vessels. Brain, heart and kidneys. The susceptibility of these organs varies from patient to patient.

In the treatment of hypertension, it is important not only to reduce the level of pressure, but also to monitor the suffering organs so that an excessive decrease in pressure does not worsen their condition even more. The selection of medical procedures and drugs for each stage of the disease should be carried out by a doctor.

At an early stage, the disease is reversible. If hypertension has developed for many years, a set of therapeutic measures can stop its development. The success of treatment is often determined by the timing of diagnosis, the correct selection of drug treatment, and compliance with all doctor's prescriptions.

Treatment The most important

condition is the observance of proper nutrition, namely the elimination from the diet of those products, which include substances that increase the level of cholesterol in the blood. First of all, this applies to high-calorie foods: meat, sweet foods (chocolate, sweets, etc.), drinks containing caffeine, etc. There are many recipes for patients with hypertension. Doctors advise such people to eat as many vegetables, fruits, and plant products as possible.

1. Drink red beet juice 1 glass 3 times a day for 2-3 weeks

2. Grate raw beetroot and mix it with flower honey (inratio 1:1). Take this mixture 1 tablespoon 3 times a day 30 minutes before meals for 3 months.

3. Mix beetroot juice (2 cups) with flower honey (1 cup), crushed lemon and carrot juice (1.5 cups). The prepared mixture should be taken 1 tablespoon 3 times a day 1 hour before meals.

4. Make a mixture of beetroot juice (1 cup), cranberries (1 cup), carrot juice (1 cup), 70% alcohol (0.5 cup) and honey (1 cup). Infuse the mixture in a dark cool place for 3 days. Prepared infusion take 1 tablespoon 3 times a day.

5. Boil potatoes in their skins and drink this decoction 1-2 cups every day. You can also eat a baked potato with the skin on.

6. Squeeze juice from 3 kg of onion, mix it with honey (500 g) and add 25 walnut films there, and then 0.5 l of vodka. Infuse this mixture for 10 days in a dark, cool place. Take ready infusion 1 tablespoon 2-3 times a day.

7. Grind and mix 3 lemons and 3 heads of garlic and pour 1 liter of boiling water. Close the container tightly and infuse for 1 day in a warm place, stirring occasionally. After that, strain the infusion. Prepared means to take 1 tablespoon 2-3 times a day 30

minutes before meals.

8. Drink daily2-3 cups of persimmon juice with pulp.

9. Every day, eat 2 cups of cranberries mixed with 3 tablespoons of sugar (1 hour before meals).

10. Crush cranberries (2 cups) and boil with sugar (0.5 cup) and water (1 cup), then strain and drink instead of tea.

Hypotension

Unlike hypertension, the main sign of hypotension is a decrease in blood pressure to 105/65–90/50 mm Hg. Art. And below.

A temporary decrease in pressure can also be observed in healthy people who often subject their body to heavy physical exertion. This is called physiological hypotension. Painful symptoms are not observed.

Physiological hypotension often occurs in athletes due to the expansion of blood vessels that supply blood to the muscles. With such hypotension, according to the Japanese, people live longer. In this case, there is no need to strive to increase the pressure. Experts call this state of high fitness hypotension.

Another type of physiological hypotension is the so-called acclimatization hypotension. It affects the inhabitants of the Far North, the tropics and subtropics, highlands. Such hypotension is also not a sign of any disease and occurs in connection with the adaptation of the whole organism, in particular blood circulation, to special loads.

Many people can live and feel great for many years with low blood pressure.

As a disease, hypotension can be acute or chronic. In acute hypotension, a person often goes into shock and fainting states. Chronic hypotension is accompanied by the development of other diseases - such as anemia, tuberculosis, dysfunction of the endocrine glands, peptic ulcer of the stomach and duodenum, tumors, heart defects, various intoxications.

Hypotension also occurs as a result of significant blood loss. Low blood pressure is observed with insufficient adrenal function and in some other conditions. To get rid of such hypotension, it is necessary first of all to treat the underlying disease, of which it is a symptom.

Often, chronic hypotension develops as a separate disease in people who have suffered mental trauma, infectious diseases, or excessive nervous tension.

Hypotension almost always accompanies acute conditions of the human body (crises): acute cardiovascular failure, anaphylactic shock (allergic crisis), etc. Crises require qualified medical care, and emergency, as they can lead to death. To quickly raise pressure and stimulate the heart muscle, there are a number of drugs that are well known to emergency doctors.

Hypotension, which is not caused by organic disorders, is entirely related to the psycho-emotional sphere. It occurs as a result of a primary dysfunction of the central nervous apparatus, which regulates vascular tone and blood pressure. It is called chronic arterial hypotension or hypotension.

The causes of this disease are different: overstrain of the central nervous system, neuro psychic trauma, physical inactivity, etc.

Arterial hypotension (hypotonic disease) occurs in the same way as hypertension due to neuroses that cause disturbances in the precise and rapid control of the work of the heart and blood vessels. Not only the causes of these diseases are similar, but in many respects even the main changes.

It is no coincidence that many patients, in their youth hypotension, with age

“Reclassified” as hypertensive patients.

Unlike hypertension, which is caused by a neurosis associated with an increase in the activity of the sympathetic department of the nervous system, hypotension is provoked by another neurosis that occurs with an increase in the function of the parasympathetic system. The predominance of the tone of the parasympathetic division of the autonomic nervous system is significantly pronounced in young patients.

While excitation of the sympathetic nervous system is associated with the release of large amounts of catecholamines into the blood, excitation of the parasympathetic nervous system leads to the release of acetylcholine, a depressant substance. Excitation and enhanced function of the parasympathetic apparatus also cause an increase in the intake of the hormone insulin into the blood, which in many respects is an antagonist of catecholamine's.

In the formation of hypotension, a certain role is played by chemical, humoral factors: a lack of pressor agents or an excess of ant pressor or depressant substances. The latter include prostaglandins A and EA, as well as kinas, especially bradykinin. One of the functions of the bradykinin apparatus in healthy people is the rapid removal of excess pressure after physical or mental stress.

Sometimes the body produces an increased amount of Brady kina. This may be due to neurosis or genetic predisposition. The increase in the production of bradykinin is also affected by long workouts or other significant physical exertion.

With hypotension, the body's adaptability to changing environmental conditions decreases. Patients do not tolerate heat, fluctuations in atmospheric pressure, strong odors, and alcoholic beverages.

They complain of lethargy, apathy, drowsiness, a feeling of severe weakness and fatigue in the morning, lack of vigor even after a long sleep, memory impairment, absent-mindedness and instability of attention. The performance of such patients is significantly reduced. They may experience a feeling of lack of air at rest, and shortness of breath appears even with little exertion. In some cases, in the evening, the legs of such patients swell.

Almost always, hypotension leads to a decrease in sexual desire, potency is disturbed in men, and the menstrual cycle is disturbed in women.

Hypotension is often accompanied by a general deterioration in mood.

Irritability and tearfulness may appear.

Sometimes the patient's only complaint is a habitual headache that occurs after sleep (often daytime) or due to fatigue disproportionate to the work done (physical or mental). Fatigue takes on the features of exhaustion. Most often, the headache covers the front temporal or front parietal region, it can be dull, pressing, constricting, bursting or pulsating and last from 2 hours to 2 days. Headache with hypertension in some cases resembles a migraine, accompanied by nausea and vomiting.

An attack of hypotension can be triggered by a sharp drop in atmospheric pressure. Sometimes it occurs as a result of a plentiful meal or a long immobile standing position, since in the first case the blood rushes to the stomach, and in the second it stagnates in the legs. Blood pressure sometimes drops in individuals who abuse caffeinated drinks such as tea or coffee.

The headache of hypotension is relieved by exposure to cold, walking in the open air, or exercise. It may stop on its own. Some patients experience headache attacks several times a day.

In addition to headache, the patient may be disturbed by dizziness and hypersensitivity to bright light, noise, loud speech. Dizziness leads to the fact that a person staggers when walking, and therefore it is difficult for him to endure being at a height, and sometimes it is not easy even to cross a bridge or street.

Hypotension can cause short-term loss of consciousness -syncope, which is considered a hypotensive crisis. Most often, fainting occurs in stuffy and hot rooms, while riding in public transport. Tall, thin men sometimes lose consciousness as a result of prolonged immobility in an upright position.

There is a so-called postural hypotension. It manifests itself in a sudden decrease in pressure after a sharp transition from a horizontal to a vertical position, which can result in fainting. Blood pressure and pulse during hypotension are very mobile, they are affected by the position of the body, time of day, mood of the patient.

A large number and variety of manifestations of low blood pressure, the absence of patterns in the course of the disease and specific symptoms do not allow hypotension to be distinguished as an independent disease. Most often, it is an external reflection of mental disorders. If neurosis is not observed, then the matter is in some unrecognized lesion of the internal organs.

Hypotension is often caused by psycho-emotional overload, so it is extremely important that everything goes smoothly in the household and industrial spheres in patients. Unfortunately, this is not always possible.

With positive emotions, the shifts caused by the violation of blood pressure, including those in the cardiovascular system, gradually disappear; negative emotions cause palpitations and vascular dysregulation, which do not disappear for a long time. Observations have shown that the pressure rises, for example, in schoolchildren at an exam at the time of taking a ticket, and gradually decreases when thinking about a question.

Passive, timid, unsure of their abilities, a little infantile, those who are afraid to take responsibility are predisposed to hypotension. For any person, especially for those predisposed to pressure violations, it is important to learn the culture of human communication in order to resolve conflicts in the gentlest way. A sense of humor helps a lot in difficult situations.

Treatment

Treatment of hypotension is carried out in three directions: normalization of impaired regulation of vascular tone, increased blood pressure and general strengthening of the body.

With the proper regimen, hypotension is eliminated, in some cases even quite quickly. Often, self-healing occurs due to the inclusion of pressure-regulating mechanisms in the patient's body.

As already mentioned, physiological hypotension does not need to be treated, but such patients are still being monitored, because low blood pressure may signal that a pathological process is occurring in some internal organs that has not yet manifested itself.

If a disease of the internal organs leading to hypotension is found, it is eliminated first of all.

Like almost all diseases, hypotension is easier to prevent than to treat. The best way to prevent is a healthy lifestyle. More on this will be discussed later.

Medical care for hypotension is as follows:

– the paticnt receives recommendations from the doctor regarding the appropriate regime of work and rest, nutrition;

– a psychotherapist conducts an active and competent treatment of neurosis.

Psychotherapy is one of the most important parts of the medical complex. Influencing the central nervous system, it also affects the autonomic nervous system, which directly regulates the level of blood pressure.

Sometimes a sufficient method is an authoritative explanation by the therapist to the patient of the nature of his illness, instilling confidence that hypotension can be dealt with, the main thing is to lead a healthy lifestyle and follow the doctor's recommendations.

Psychotherapists should actively influence the neurosis, who will help strengthen the patient's volitional sphere, teach him a number of auto-training techniques, apply hypnosis methods, if necessary, etc.

The state of mind of a person is largely depends on the psychological climate that is created by him and those around him in any living conditions.

The doctor will help him understand the situation and find a way to resolve the conflict, to exclude emotional stress from relationships with people.

The treatment complex for hypotension includes various physiotherapeutic procedures: electro and phono psoriasis, hydrotherapy. Some patients are prescribed sodium chloride, carbon dioxide, and hydrogen sulfide, oxygen baths, which actively affect vascular tone and control the nervous system of the circulatory apparatus.

In the treatment of hypotension, proper nutrition gives a good effect. In extreme cases, you can use medications that belong to two groups:

– psychotropic - those that affect the central nervous system; anti-anxiety medications, such as sleeping pills;

– Means that directly increase the release of blood from the heart or the tone of arterioles, and therefore increase blood pressure to the required level. The latter include the well-known caffeine, Citroen, caffeine, ask fen, etc.

A large number of stimulants of the body, which, by increasing the general tone, increase the pressure, came to scientific medicine from folk medicine. Communication with nature is very useful for hypotensive patients, so at least regular walks in the park are recommended. One day a week or half a day must be spent outdoors, especially if the work takes place indoors.

It is useful for hypotensive patients to regularly visit a bath or sauna, in a hot atmosphere in which pressure rises. Hypertensive patients, especially at the 3rd stage, cannot do this.

Diet for patients with hypotension

There is no special diet for patients suffering from low blood pressure. They can eat whatever they want, trying not to overeat. Very often patients with hypotension drink strong tea or coffee. Tea, coffee, cocoa and chocolate contain caffeine - a substance that has a stimulating effect on the nervous system, increases the release of blood from the heart and the tone of the arterioles, resulting in an increase in blood pressure.

An indisputable fact is the relationship between the level of blood pressure and the use of table salt (sodium chloride). This was also confirmed by experiments on animals, when an excess of salt caused an increase in pressure (salt hypertension), and when it was excluded from the diet, the previously elevated pressure decreased. For comparison, residents of Greenland and Japan were examined. Greenlanders consume 4 g of salt per day, their pressure averages 90/70 mm Hg. Art. The daily diet of the Japanese includes up to 15 g of salt, their average pressure is 170/100 mm Hg. Art. For this reason, the diet of patients with hypotension in the first place Characterized by an increase in the content of salt in food.

Salt increases pressure due to sodium ions, the opposite effect is exerted by potassium ions. Potassium and magnesium, necessary to improve the functioning of the heart and blood vessels, are found in carrots, dill, parsley, dried apricots, raisins, citrus fruits.

A single diet for all patients with hypotension does not exist. It depends on age, profession, and lifestyle and, first of all, should be determined by how much energy is consumed by a particular person. It can only be argued that for those who are engaged in heavy physical labor, the norm of food consumption should be 2-3 times higher than for people with moderate mental labor.

Limit calorie intake by avoiding foods that contain animal fats (for example, fatty meats and fish, sausages) and carbohydrates (especially net carbohydrates - sugar, confectionery and flour products, cereals, legumes, and potatoes). However, the diet must include a sufficient amount of complete proteins (lean meats, poultry, fish and dairy products), which help improve metabolism and reduce water retention in the body. It is also impossible to completely refuse carbohydrates, the absence of which leads to the development of a pathological condition - acidosis.

To eliminate the feeling of hunger with a low-calorie diet and suppress appetite, it is recommended to eat small meals, but often: 5-6 times a day.

Periodic fasting days are very effective. Here are their sample meals.

Meat day: 450 g lean unsalted meat, 500 g sauerkraut, 2-3 cups rosehip broth (no sugar).

Apple day: 1.5 kg of apples (300 g in 5 doses).

Compote day: dried fruit compote (250 g per 1 liter of water) without sugar (possible with xylitol).

Cottage cheese day: 600 g low-fat cottage cheese, 100 ml milk.

On a fasting day, it is desirable to reduce physical activity. The following dishes and products are recommended for consumption:

– wheat bread from flour of I and II grades, bran bread of yesterday's baking;

– soups, mostly vegetarian, from cereals and vegetables, as well as dairy, fruit; beetroot;

– meat, poultry (lean beef, pork, veal, chicken, boiled turkey, in pieces or chopped, baked after boiling);

– low-fat varieties of fish (boiled or fried after boiling, chopped in the form of meatballs, meatballs,

meatballs);

– Milk and dairy products: natural milk, sour-milk drinks, low-fat cottage cheese and products made from it (cheesecakes, lazy dumplings, casseroles). Sour cream only for dressing;

– eggs (1 soft-boiled egger in the form of a steam protein omelet);

– cereals(cereals on water or milk, puddings and cereals);

– any finely chopped vegetables in boiled, baked and raw form; leafy greens; exclude legumes, radishes, pickled, pickled and salted vegetables;

– fresh fruits and berries; compotes, kisses, mousses, jelly, juices; dried fruits;

– Sauces on vegetable broth, as well as milk and sour cream; sweet fruit sauces; Drinks - weak tea and coffee.

Important in the prevention of hypotension is the observance of some general principles of nutrition. You have to eat slowly. The feeling of fullness occurs after about 20 minutes, so when eating in a hurry, you can eat more food, still feeling hungry.

It is necessary to eat at certain hours in order to form conditioned reflexes. It is important to eat 3-4 times a day or more often in small portions. It is very harmful to eat on the go, in a hurry.

For the treatment of hypotension, it is recommended to take some decoctions and tinctures prepared according to traditional medicine recipes.

Immortelle tincture

Pour 1 cup boiling water over 10 g of dried immortelle flowers. Let it brew. Take 25 drops daily in the morning and at lunchtime before meals.

Tartar tincture

Pour 5 tablespoons of prickly tartar leaves with 5 cups of steep, leave for 2-3 hours, cool and strain. Take orally 6 times a day for 0.25 cups.

Decoction of immortelle

Pour 10–15 g of dried immortelle flowers with 1 glass of water. Put on fire and boil for 3-5 minutes. Remove from heat, cool and strain. Take daily for 3 weeks, 3 times a day, and 20-30 minutes before meals.

Fragrant infusion

Take crushed herbs: 1 part of Veronica officinalis, wild strawberry and common chicory 7 parts of St. John's wort, 2 parts of fragrant rue and common yarrow.

Mix herbs, add 2 parts of cinnamon rose hips and crushed medicinal lavage root, 0.25 parts of juniper fruits and 0.25 parts of marsh clams rhizome. Pour 3 tablespoons of the resulting mixture into a thermos, pour 0.25 liters of boiling water and leave for 10–12 hours. Divide the finished infusion into 3 parts and take it orally throughout the day, 20–30 minutes before meals.

Thistle infusion

Pour 1 cup of boiling water over 1 tablespoon of thistle leaves, infuse for 3-4 hours, strain and refrigerate. Take 3 times a day for 0.25 cups.

Tatar juice

Squeeze juice from fresh leaves of the prickly tartar and take it orally 3 times a day, 1/2-1 teaspoon.

Prickly tartar powder

Peel the dry leaves of the tartar from thorns, grind until a powdery mass is obtained. The resulting substance is taken orally 3 times a day, 0.25-1 teaspoon.

Tincture of lure high

Prepare a tincture of 40% alcohol, roots and rhizomes of a high lure in a ratio of 5: 1. Take 40 drops daily 2 times a day.

A decoction of inflorescences and leaves of prickly tartar

Pour 20-25 g of dry leaves and inflorescences of prickly tartar with 1 cup of hot water, put on low heat and boil for 10 minutes. Then pour the broth into a closed vessel, wrap with a warm cloth and leave for 30 minutes. After that, strain, cool and take 3 times a day, 1 tablespoon.

Lemongrass tincture

Prepare a tincture of 70% alcohol and Chinese lemongrass mixed in a ratio of 10: 1. Take 2 times a day 20–30 minutes before meals, 30–35 drops per 0.25 glass of water.

Aralia tincture

Prepare a tincture of 70% alcohol and aralia root Manchurian in a ratio of 5: 1. Take daily for 1-2 months, 3-4 times a day, 40-50 drops.

Summer infusion

Take crushed herbs: 1 part of dyeing gorse, knotweed, medicinal verbena and peppermint, 2 parts of narrow-leaved fireweed, common oregano, large plantain, and ivy-shaped board, 7 parts of St. John's wort.

Mix chopped herbs add 0.25 parts of the rhizome of calamus, and common juniper fruits and 3 parts of cinnamon rose hips.

Place 5–6 tablespoons of the finished mixture in a thermos, pour 1 liter of boiling water, close the lid tightly and let it brew for 7–10 hours. Drink the finished infusion 2 days 3 times a day 30 minutes before meals.

Infusion mixed

Take crushed herbs and leaves: 2 parts of Veronica officinalis, white birch leaves, 1 part of hyssop officinalis, dioica nettle, horsetail, black currant leaves, 0.25 parts of peppermint and wild strawberry leaves, 5 parts of prickly tartar.

Grind 2 parts of dandelion root and 0.25 parts of high elecampane rhizome.

Mix 3 parts of cinnamon rose hips, 2 parts of ordinary mordovnik fruits, add crushed herbs, leaves and chopped roots.

Place 4-5 tablespoons of the prepared mixture in a thermos, pour 1 liter of boiling water and leave for 12 hours. Take the prepared infusion inside 2 days 3 times a day 30 minutes before meals.

Birch infusion

Take crushed herbs and leaves: 3 parts of white birch leaves, 1 part of ivy-shaped board, leaves of large plantain and common yarrow, 2 parts of stinging nettle, knotweed,

7 parts of prickly tartar. Mix 2 parts each of cinnamon rose hips and wild strawberries, add crushed herbs and leaves, as well as crushed 0.25 parts of high elecampane rhizome.

Pour 3 tablespoons of the prepared mixture into a thermos, pour 0.25 liters of boiling water and leave for 10 hours. Take the prepared infusion inside 3 times a day on an empty stomach 20–30 minutes before meals.

Infusion of a mixture of herbs

Take crushed herbs and leaves: 1 part of Veronica officinalis, narrow-leaved fireweed, peppermint leaves, fragrant rue, 5 parts each Hypercom perforated and prickly tartar, Mix 2 parts of the fruits of the common mordrevnik, cinnamon rose hips, add crushed herbs and leaves, crushed 1 part of the roots and rhizomes of elecampane and 0.25 parts of the marsh calamus rhizome.

Pour 6 tablespoons of the finished mixture into a thermos and pour 1 liter of boiling water. Infuse for 10–12 hours. Take the prepared infusion inside for 2 days, 3 times a day, 30–40 minutes before meals.

Chapter 4

Such diseases include a group of diseases in which various mental disorders are observed. At the same time, functional changes in mental activity occur. In the case of neurosis, there is no distortion of the reflection of the real picture of the world, while in psychosis, an adequate assessment of reality is violated.

Withdrawal hangover syndrome in alcoholism

Chronic alcoholism is classified as a mental illness. It occurs as a result of prolonged intoxication of the body with alcohol. In this case, damage to the internal organs and the brain occurs. Pathological addiction to taking ethyl alcohol leads to the fact that the disease gradually progresses, leading to aggravation of forms of alcohol intoxication, to mental and physical health disorders and the appearance of withdrawal symptoms.

There are 3 main stages in the development of alcoholism.

At the first stage, the appearance of a pathological craving for alcohol. He patient loses control over quantity drunk, intoxication is often manifested in severe forms accompanied by amnesia. Abstinence (hangover syndrome) at this stage is not observed. A person who is in the initial stage of the disease does not vomit after taking significant doses of alcohol. Mental manifestations in this period connected Sastenia, drops sentiments with the predominance of downgrades, irritability, high fatigue and low performance, signs of self-doubt. This stage the disease can last 3-6 years.

At the second stage of alcoholism, an increase in dependence on alcohol and the appearance of a pronounced withdrawal syndrome are observed.

During this period, the patient is

characterized by uncontrolled and uncontrollable craving for alcoholic products. He can be in many days of continuous drunkenness. Pseudo-binge drinking may occur. Working capacity decreases even more, fatigue increases under load.

Changes in the character of the patient are also noted: such traits as rudeness, deceit, selfishness begin to appear. Intellectual abilities, like memory, the ability to critically evaluate are significantly reduced. There is an imbalance in the emotional sphere, characterized by the emergence of a tendency to hysteria, incontinence. The second period can last 7–20 years. The third stage of the disease is considered especially severe. It is characterized by true binges lasting for 1 week or longer. This is followed by a break followed by a period of drinking. Intoxication occurs very quickly, while the smallest doses of alcohol are enough. Patients are no longer forced to take vodka, but fortified cheap wines, various surrogates.

During this period, there is an increase in the symptoms of the disease, characteristic of the second stage. In addition, the hangover syndrome becomes more pronounced. At the same time, strong somatic vegetative disorders are the result of severe intoxication. The degradation of the personality is revealed. At this stage, somatic disorders occur: chronic gastritis, kidney and liver damage, hypertension and alcoholic cardiopathy. Alcoholic psychosis, epileptiform seizures are not excluded. Neurological disorders develop: autonomic dystonia, impaired tendon reflexes, and in some cases polyneuritis.

In the last stages of the disease, asthenic syndrome can manifest itself in the form of sleep disorders, mild depression, dyspepsia, etc. These disorders are also observed for several months after stopping the use of alcoholic beverages.

Various emotions - such as anger, joy, and grief sick people experience more intensely than healthy people. Their reactions to events become affective and explosive.

This is due to the appearance of the so-called alcoholic character, which begins to form from the beginning of the second stage of the disease, then worsens. There are neurotic and psychopathic personality changes. Against the background of increased fatigue, increased excitability and a tendency to hypochondria, which takes on the character of various phobias, are noted.

One of the most noticeable symptoms that appear in the third stage of the disease are memory disorders, often aggravated by the addition of vascular disorders or cranial cerebral injuries.

With alcoholism in men, the cardiovascular system is more often affected, while women are more likely to suffer from disorders of the liver and gastrointestinal tract.

Gradually, alcohol abuse leads a person to social and mental degradation. He completely loses his professional qualifications, is forced to switch first to low-skilled work, then to odd jobs, after which he loses his job, his lifestyle becomes parasitic. As a rule, the patient comes to such a finale after the age of 40.

As already mentioned, one of the consequences of the excessive use of alcoholic beverages is the withdrawal syndrome, which mainly occurs in the second stage of alcoholism and lasts about 2 weeks or longer. In the first stage of the disease, it can last for several days.

A similar condition of the patient can be observed in the period from 2 to 15 years after the onset of alcohol abuse. The painful state of a hangover manifests itself the next day after drinking alcohol in the form of mental and somatic disorders.

A patient with a hangover has a rapid pulse, asthenic disorders. He suffers from headache, dizziness and heart pain. This condition is characterized by weakness and weakness, tremor of the limbs (mainly of the hands), a feeling of cold. In some cases, patients experience muscle pain, constant thirst. At the same time, such manifestations as a decrease in appetite are observed, vomiting, nausea and diarrhea, pain in the abdomen and liver may occur. A hangover is accompanied by a violation of night sleep.

For adolescence (13-17 years), the onset of withdrawal syndrome can be observed after 1-3 years of regular alcohol abuse, but even before the onset of signs of a hangover, adolescents often drink for several days to several weeks in a row. The disease becomes pronounced in this case after about 2-5 years. As a rule, changes in the personality of a young person develop rapidly and become apathetic. Often, young people suffering from alcoholism begin to use barbiturates.

Women who are prone to alcoholism begin to feel a hangover syndrome 3 years after the onset of the disease. At the same time, a clear predominance of mental disorders over somatic ones is noted. Women suffer from depression more often than men.

Symptoms of poor health are relieved by alcoholics by taking small doses of alcohol. Gradually, they have to switch to drinking alcohol not only in the morning, but also during the day, repeating this procedure several times.

The fact that the attraction to alcohol has already acquired the character of life necessity (and not just dependence) and reached its maximum is evidenced by the following undoubted sign. It lies in the fact that on the 3rd-4th day, one can state the apogee of the severity of abstinence.

In medical practice, rarer cases have been noted when a patient consumes fractional doses of alcohol, without taking breaks between binges. In this case, the withdrawal syndrome simply does not have time to develop.

Treatment

Modern medicine has a variety of methods and medications for the successful treatment of alcoholism and withdrawal symptoms. However, treatment, especially at the last stage of the disease, is much more difficult than preventing it. A significant role here is played by abstinence from immoderate frequent consumption of alcoholic beverages, a healthy lifestyle and proper nutrition, which allow avoiding a painful addiction to alcohol.

If domestic drunkenness has already led to prolonged intoxication of the body with alcohol and to the emergence of alcoholism as a mental illness, all possible means should be used to restore health.

As a rule, all people suffering from alcoholism eat poorly. They do not pay due attention to the diversity of their diet and the content of the necessary amount of nutrients in it. Attention of patients in the last stages of the disease, attract only alcoholic beverages, as a result, the body receives less vital substances and compounds.

Despite the fact that alcohol is quite high in calories, it does not contain nutrients. A person who abuses alcohol gets a lot of calories and because of this loses his appetite for other foods. When using the calories of alcohol, the cells require nutrients and spend them from reserve reserves, quickly depleting them. The body as a whole weakens, which affects the work of not only internal organs, but also mental processes.

That is why people who are addicted to alcohol need to change their attitude to the quality and quantity of food. As a result, the development of the disease can be stopped.

Often the problem is that many alcoholics do not consider themselves sick and do not recognize the need for treatment. Therefore, the first step on the path to health is associated with an explanatory work that is carried out in the family and with the help of psychotherapists, neurologists, psychiatrists.

Treatment is carried out both in the hospital and on an outpatient basis. It depends on several factors: the desire of the patient, on his physical and mental condition. In severe withdrawal syndrome, in the presence of psychotic manifestations, with obvious mental and somatic disorders, treatment in a hospital is indicated.

The process of medical treatment should be accompanied by a proper vitamin-rich high-calorie diet. If the patient is severely malnourished, he is prescribed insulin in small doses to increase his appetite.

It has a beneficial effect on the general condition of a person suffering alcoholism, drinking plenty of juices, mineral water, fruit drinks, and herbal teas. At the same time, diuretics are prescribed.

Along with restorative treatment with high-calorie foods rich in minerals, psychotherapy is constantly carried out. It should contribute to the development of a positive attitude in the patient to the treatment process and sobriety. Establishing the necessary contact with the attending physician, trust, mutual understanding and belief in the possibility of a successful recovery are of paramount importance for the effectiveness of treatment efforts.

In addition, conditioned reflex therapy is used as one of the methods of treatment. It consists in the development and consolidation of a conditioned reflex in the form of nausea and vomiting from the smell or taste of alcohol. Usually resort to a maximum of 20-25 sessions.

Treatment using various methods can take quite a long time. During this period, patients experience suffering from the manifestation of the same vegetative and mental disorders that are observed with a hangover (irritability, nervous breakdowns, anxiety, etc.). These disorders (pseudo-withdrawal syndrome) occur against the background of sobriety and push a person to relapse into use. Alcohol. Here it is especially important to give the patient support, understanding and prevent a breakdown. Doctors in this case usually give their recommendations.

But the easiest and most affordable way to remove the craving for alcohol in each case of its occurrence is to eat tasty and hearty. With a feeling of satiety in the stomach, the desire to drink almost disappears. Most likely, you will need to take sedatives (phenazepam, seduxen, sonapax) until the addiction disappears.

By resorting to clinical nutrition and some proven means, you can help not only the patient, but also his relatives who are faced with the problem of alcohol addiction in the family. It must be remembered that:

1. First of all, in order to avoid severe intoxication, doctors and traditional medicine recommend drinking a cup of green or black well-brewed mint tea. Black coffee or tea with lemon can have the same effect that prevents rapid intoxication. In this case, lemon added to tea or coffee has a neutralizing effect on alcohol. To remove mild intoxication, if it occurs, immediately after the feast, doctors recommend repeating the procedure.

2. It should be borne in mind that severe intoxication, which has the

most negative consequences, occurs as a result of drinking a mixture of different varieties of wine and vodka. In this case, a person's well-being becomes several times worse than when using any one type of alcoholic beverage.

3. Metabolic processes play an important role in the life of the body. In the event of psychosis on the basis of alcoholism, vitamin therapy is carried out. Many fruits are a rich source of vitamins and have a beneficial effect on alcohol poisoning.

One of the most effective ways to eliminate a hangover is to use persimmons. It contains fructose, and vitamins A and C are contained in a combination that allows you to get good results in the fight against the manifestations of the disease.

In clinical nutrition, doctors recommend introducing lemon as well. It has a pronounced antitoxic, soothing effect. If you eat a whole lemon fruit before drinking alcohol, you can avoid intoxication of the body.

With a hangover, it is recommended to drink tea with lemon, using 1-2 fruits during the day. This fruit contains many useful substances, including B vitamins, especially indicated for withdrawal symptoms. Lemon in large doses can be consumed if there are no contraindications from the gastrointestinal tract.

4. To quickly restore health with a hangover, doctors recommend eating quince and oranges. It is advisable to supplement the consumption of fruits with injections of a complex of essential vitamins.

5. Research conducted at the Tokyo Center for Nutrition and aimed at finding optimal medicinal products to combat withdrawal, confirm the effectiveness of the use of fruits and fruit drinks, which allows them to be recommended as the best remedy, since

fruits contain natural fructose.

Due to the fact that this substance helps to speed up the metabolism, the process of processing excess alcohol by the body is activated, which leads to a rapid normalization of the human condition.

6. As a sobering agent, you can successfully use mint water (20 drops of mint herb tincture in 1 glass of chilled water). This solution is recommended to drink as soon as possible after drinking alcohol. The tool not only relieves intoxication, but also a feeling of heaviness, pain in the head.

7. In case of alcohol poisoning, they induce vomiting with a cup of hot coffee, to which it is recommended to add table salt instead of sugar.

8. The next day after a strong intoxication, as a rule, intoxication of the body occurs, resulting in unpleasant sensations in the stomach, headache. In

this case, the patient is given to drink 1 glass of beer and his back, chest and face are rubbed with ice. In this case, a trip to the bath should be considered an effective remedy.

9. For very severe headaches, it is enough to drink 1 glass of cucumber pickle. If the day before a person was not abstinent not only in taking alcohol, but also in the amount of food eaten, doctors recommend the whole next day to refrain from eating anything, with the exception of fruits. It is useful to spend the day in bed, putting a heating pad on your stomach.

10. In case of alcohol poisoning, sprouted beans, eaten, provide effective help.

11. With a hangover syndrome, sour-milk drinks "Tan" or "Aryan" help well. With alcoholism (if there are no contraindications, for example, in connection with a stomach ulcer), garlic can be used in food not only as an

antitoxic agent, but to increase appetite.

12. In folk medicine, the morel saprophyte fungus is used as food. It has a beneficial effect on the state of the gastrointestinal tract, stimulates appetite, and is a general tonic.

A medicinal decoction of mushrooms is also used. To prepare it, take fresh mushrooms (1 tablespoon), pour 1 cup of boiling water, boil 30 min, insist for 4 hours. Then the broth is filtered. Take it 4 times a day, 0.25 cups 10-15 minutes before meals.

In chronic alcoholism, infusions and decoctions of herbs provide significant assistance. Some of the recipes have a curative effect, with the help of others you can create an aversion to drinking alcohol.

1. A decoction of bearberry is prepared as follows: grass leaves (2 tablespoons) are brewed with a glass of boiling water and boiled for 15 minutes.

Take 5-6 times a day, 1 tablespoon.

2. To prepare the next infusion, you should use a mixture of herbs taken in equal parts: centaury, thyme and wormwood. Three tablespoons of ingredients are placed in a thermos, poured

1 glass of boiling water, insist 2 hours, after which the infusion is filtered. Take 4 times a day, 1 tablespoon per day.

3. Craving for alcohol is significantly reduced by the daily consumption of sour varieties of apples.

4. In some cases, healing from alcoholism occurs as a result of treating the patient with bee venom.

5. In the treatment of alcoholism, you can use warm herbal infusions instead of tea. They are consumed daily in large quantities (10-15 glasses a day), without sugar and with strict abstinence from alcohol.

This treatment is beneficial influence on the body, especially on the stomach and blood composition. The tea may be made up of equal parts St. John's wort, yarrow, wormwood and mint; you can take 0.25 parts of juniper berries, angelica root and calamus root. All components are mixed and brewed with 1 glass of water, like tea, taking 2 tablespoons without top.

Aversion to alcohol causes the use of the following recipes used, as a rule, with a small amount of alcohol.

1. Laurel noble (2 leaves) and lavage root are poured with 1 glass of vodka. The infusion is kept for 2 weeks and given to the patient to drink.

2. Dry chopped grass of the marsh ram (10 g) is poured with 1 glass of boiling water, the container is put on fire and boiled for 20-30 minutes. The decoction is drunk 70-100 g per day. This prescription should be used only after consulting a physician, who must

determine whether there are any contraindications to the use of the remedy for this patient.

3. Herb thyme or creeping thyme, (15 g) is poured with 1 cup of boiling water and infused for 15 minutes. Drink infusion 3 times a day, 1tablespoon.

Taking a 75% decoction of thyme in large quantities simultaneously with alcohol causes an emetic reaction. However, such treatment of alcoholism has contraindications.

Doctors do not recommend this remedy during pregnancy, ill ness kidneys and liver, severe atherosclerosis of cerebral vessels, cardiosclerosis, individual intolerance, gastric and duodenal ulcers, pre-infarction state, and atrial fibrillation.

4. You can prepare a simple folk remedy that averts the use of alcohol. To do this, put a few green forest bugs

in vodka, emitting an unpleasant pungent odor (they are collected from raspberry bushes, where they are sometimes found), insist 1 day, filter the vodka and offer the patient. You should not tell him about the method of preparing the drink.

5. It is necessary to prepare and take the next decoction with exact dosage, because the plant is poisonous.

Crushed hoof root (1 tablespoon) is poured with a glass of water and boiled over low heat for 10 minutes.

Then the broth is poured into a thermos (or wrapped), incubated for 30 minutes, filtered. A tablespoon of the product is added to 200 g of vodka and given to a person suffering from alcohol addiction to drink, without telling him about the composition. Drinking causes vomiting and aversion to alcohol.

In addition to using the above food remedies, some other ways to deal with the consequences of excessive alcohol consumption are also used.

To quickly sober up a slightly intoxicated person, he is given to drink 200 g of cold water, to which 2 drops of ammonia are added. This remedy also helps with severe intoxication, in which case the amount of ammonia is increased to 5-6 drops. This solution can be carefully poured into the mouth of a person who is in a deep degree of intoxication.

An effective way to restore the full consciousness of a heavily intoxicated person without the slightest harm to health has long been known and used in the East. To do this, you need to rub the auricles of a drunkard strongly and quickly. A few minutes later, he will come to his senses and even be able to speak coherently.

It should be remembered that if, after taking alcohol, you go outside in the winter (or other cold time), the state of intoxication can significantly increase under the influence of cold fresh air. AT In some cases, there is even loss of consciousness.

If a patient with alcoholism is in a state of binge, and at the same time his behavior becomes inadequate and violent, acquiring an asocial character, you should seek medical help, which he will be provided in a hospital. You can resort to the following measures: pour cold water over your head, put mustard plasters on the back of your head, and make cool baths (water should be at room temperature).

Neuroses

This is the name of a complex of diseases that are based on temporary disturbances of mental activity that are functional in nature. They can occur as a result of overstrain of nervous processes under the influence of a prolonged traumatic situation (stress, overwork), when the body is exposed to certain harmful substances, and also due to internal pathological processes.

The manifestations of neuroses are different. At the same time, mental exhaustion is noted, a deterioration in the general well-being of the patient, a violation of some vegetative somatic functions of the body is observed.

As a rule, neurosis manifests itself in 4 main forms: neurasthenia, hysteria, obsessive-compulsive disorder and hypochondriacally neurosis.

Neurasthenia may be the result of nervous exhaustion under the influence of a traumatic situation, prolonged lack of rest. It is characterized by irritability in combination with increased fatigue, neuro psychic weakness, and sleep disturbances. With neurasthenia, increased sweating, shortness of breath, palpitations and discomfort in the region of the heart are observed.

Malnutrition is an important factor contributing to the onset of the disease.

Patients suffering from neurasthenia quickly get tired at any load, they are prone to sudden mood swings, and complacency can easily be replaced by depression. With this disease, the nervous reaction to the most insignificant unpleasant or unfriendly words is intensified, causing irritation and affective reactions. Neurasthenics suffer from a disturbance in the process of falling asleep, complaining of superficial sleep, which tends to be interrupted frequently. After waking up, patients often feel a headache, a state of weakness. With neurasthenia, general somatic and vegetative disorders are noted.

The development of the disease has 3 stages: hypersthene, transitional and hyposthenia.

The hypersthene stage is

characterized by a high degree of irritability, while an unrestrained and intolerant character is observed, and obvious attention disorders are noted. With an exacerbation diseases mark confusion of thoughts (asthenic mentism).

The transitional stage of the disease state is characterized by the so-called irritable weakness. Neurasthenics show explosive reactions, but after that they feel severe weakness, sometimes apathy, drowsiness. Sleep helps restore strength. In this stage of the disease, neurasthenics, as a rule, do not complete the work due to rapidly growing fatigue.

The third stage (hyposthenia) is more characterized by symptoms of mental and physical asthenia. Intellectual activity is accompanied by particularly rapid fatigue and lethargy. It becomes difficult for patients to perform any kind of physical work. Activity continues to fall and is practically not manifested, being replaced by lethargy and drowsiness.

With neurasthenia, a very painful reaction to noise, bright light, and sudden changes in temperature is observed.

Autonomic disorders are also noted - such as profuse sweating, weakness, heart palpitations, lowering the temperature of the legs and hands. Patients report a throbbing headache that makes it difficult to concentrate. Neurasthenics are touchy, they often cry, they develop hypochondriacally tendencies. All these factors prevent these people from working productively.

When carrying out treatment and changing the situation, which patients perceive as traumatic, a quick recovery of the patient can occur.

Hysteria can have a different clinical picture. With this form of neurosis, vegetative and somatic disorders are observed, in particular, violations of the respiratory function, as well as the work of the cardiovascular system and the digestive tract. Not infrequently, a violation of the sensitivity of the arms, legs, chest, as well as motor functions, etc. However, these deviations are the result of self-hypnosis, and not the pathology of the work of internal organs or any systems.

Sometimes hysteria manifests itself in the form of hysterical fits, which can only occur in the presence of spectators and have a bright external design. After a seizure, amnesia of a greater or lesser degree is sometimes stated, which is temporary.

During hysterical attacks, patients often weep for a long time, talk about unbearable suffering and do everything they can to draw attention to the desperation of their situation. Sometimes, against the background of a seizure, temporary blindness, hypertensive crises develop, dumbness or deafness. It can be said that patients try to find refuge from traumatic problems, unpleasant everyday situations and do not want to make any effort to get rid of this condition. The selfish and demonstrative behavior of a person suffering from hysteria (more often a woman than a man) is aimed at achieving the set goals.

Compulsive neurosis physicians refer to the most common diseases. It manifests itself in the fact that patients have obsessive fears, thoughts, and doubts. Patients are insecure, prone to introspection, vulnerable and highly sensitive. They may develop a fear of heights, a fear of closed spaces, a fear of transport, etc. Sometimes patients may complain of the appearance of intrusive accounts, rearrangements of objects, and memories of negative content. Patients are critical of these manifestations, they spend a lot of mental strength on the fight against obsessions, but they cannot get rid of them.

The content of obsessions may be associated with fears associated with assumptions about the presence of an incurable or shameful disease in those suffering from neurosis. This may include, for example, the fear of being hit by AIDS, syphilis, cancer, etc. With the patient fully understanding that he cannot have serious reasons for the development of such diseases, he notices that his thoughts still constantly continue to return to this topic.

Any assumption can take possession of a person and constantly pursue him. For example, a neurosis may be manifested by the patient's sudden assumption that his relative was buried alive. He tries to drive away these thoughts, tells himself that this cannot be, but thoughts about it keep coming back obsessively.

Sometimes obsessive-compulsive disorder may be associated with a person's insistence on committing an antisocial act. By a person subject to this kind of neurosis, his own ideas, impulses and proposed actions are evaluated as unacceptable, absolutely unlawful and terrible. For example, an unbearable desire to do something obscene (swear in a public place, insult a respected person) or a mother's desire to drown her child in a bathtub bring suffering to the patient, since these aspirations are in deep conflict with his upbringing and moral principles.

In order to refrain from their unnatural desires, patients are forced to make great efforts,This form of obsessive-compulsive disorder affects people who are suspicious, indecisive and prone to anxiety.

Hypochondriacally neurosis characterizes the painful attention of a person suffering from it to their own health. Patients cannot get rid of suspicions and beliefs that they are seriously ill. They visit different doctors to find confirmation of their thoughts, but doctors do not find any deviations and terrible diseases. However, persons suffering from hypochondriacally neurosis experience discomfort in their body, similar to the symptoms of certain diseases. At the same time, patients often have a depressed depressive mood.

Treatment

The main conditions for recovery from neurosis are the establishment of a healthy lifestyle, regular rest and sleep, as well as the elimination of a traumatic situation, the necessary treatment and proper nutrition.

Along with psycho- and physiotherapy for patients, By eliminating factors that contribute to the appearance of tension and anxiety, one should streamline the daily routine of a person suffering from any form of neurosis. This is especially true when it comes to rest. Sleep must be complete. Doctors recommend that all patients of this group eat well and regularly, be sure to take vitamins. As a treatment, measures should be taken to strengthen the body in general.

In many forms of neurosis, general nervous excitement is removed with the help of herbal medicine. Doctors recommend using the following remedies, infusions, decoctions and juices.

1. The crushed roots of the herb valerian officinalis (1 tablespoon), pour 1 cup of boiled cold water, insist for 6-8 hours, then filter. Take 1 tablespoon of infusion 3 times a day.

2. You can also prepare an infusion of valerian officinalis in another way. Take the crushed grass root (1 teaspoon), pour 1 cup of boiling water, leave for 20 minutes. Take 1 glass of infusion hot, before going to bed.

The course of taking valerian is limited2 months

3. Valerian decoction is prepared by pouring the crushed herb root (1 tablespoon) into 1 cup of hot water. The liquid is boiled for 15 minutes. Decoction is recommended to be taken 3 times a day, 1 tablespoon.

4. Freshly squeezed motherwort herb juice is taken 30-40 drops each 3-4 times a day 30 minutes before meals.

5. To prepare the infusion, take motherwort herb (1-2 tablespoons), pour 1 cup of boiling water and insist until the liquid cools down, then filter the infusion. Motherwort infusion should be taken 20 minutes before meals, 1-2 tablespoons 3 to 5 times a day.

6. Common yarrow herb(1 teaspoon) pour 1 cup of boiling water, filter and take 1 time per day. The amount of infusion can be increased

from 1 tablespoon to 0.3 cups, depending on the patient's condition.

7. The following infusion is used for vegetative neuroses. Pre-pounded dry blood-red hawthorn fruits (1 tablespoon) are placed in a thermos and brewed with 1 glass of hot water. Insist for 2 hours, filter. The infusion should be taken before meals 3-4 times a day, 1-2 tablespoons.

8. With neurasthenia, headache and insomnia, 2 tablespoons of willow-herb or fireweed are poured with 2 cups of boiling water. Insist in the oven or thermos for 6 hours, filter. Drink the infusion 3-4 times during the day, dividing it into equal portions.

9. As a sedative, an infusion of common viburnum is used. To prepare it, viburnum fruits are ground in a mortar, take 5 tablespoons of raw materials and pour 3 cups of boiling water, insist in a thermos for 4 hours, filter. Take 0.5 cup before meals 4-5

times a day.

10. Spring young birch leaves (100 g) are crushed, poured with 2 cups of boiled warm water, infused for 5–6 hours. Then the mass is filtered, squeezed, settled, and poured to remove sediment. The infusion is drunk before meals 2-3 times a day for 0.5 cups.

In case of excessive temper and irritability, tinctures of valerian herb, lily of the valley should be taken, while ginseng and lemongrass should be used to stimulate nervous and psychophysical processes.

Those suffering from hysteria need to resort to vitamin therapy. Fruits or vegetables should be present in their daily diet. Physiotherapeutic procedures and spa treatment have a beneficial effect for these patients.

Nutrition should be complete, regular and orderly. It is necessary to normalize the mode of eating. Doctors also recommend avoiding overeating.

Patients with obsessive-compulsive disorder should limit the use of excessively spicy, irritating food. It is better to exclude spicy seasonings from the diet and do not abuse dishes containing fresh onions and garlic. Doctors recommend focusing on well-being when choosing hot spices.

With phobias, the correct regimen of the day, good sleep is especially important. The last meal should consist of light meals (vegetable salads, lactic acid drinks) and take place no later than 4 hours before bedtime. With the provision of normal sleep, worries and fears lose their intensity and torment.

Irritability can be combated with salty pine baths and warm foot baths at night, which have a relaxing effect.

With all types of neurosis, daily honey intake (no more than 100-140 g per day) is of exceptional benefit. It is also recommended to eat other bee products (perga, royal jelly).

With neurosis and depression, a mixture of royal jelly with honey (1: 100) can have a beneficial effect. The remedy is taken three times a day, 1 teaspoon, kept in the mouth until dissolved.

With neuroses, taking a mixture of honey and pollen (1: 1) helps, if taken daily, 1 teaspoon 3 times a day.

With insomnia, natural honey is a very effective remedy. It also brings general benefits to the body. In 1 glass of warm water, stir 1 tablespoon of natural honey and drink 30 minutes before bedtime.

Mental disorders in traumatic brain injury

As a result of traumatic brain injury, mental disorders can occur. They are caused by mechanical damage to the substance of the brain of varying severity.

These mental disorders are distinguished depending on several factors. The severity of the injury, the presence of blood loss, localization, damage to other internal organs, the presence of intoxication or infections associated with the injury are taken into account.

Poor oxygen supply to the brain during bleeding (hemorrhage) contributes to impaired blood circulation, as well as the occurrence of psychoses that are acute. Increased capillary permeability leads to cerebral edema, while the features of the manifestation of the nature of psychosis largely depend on the degree of edema.

Intracranial hemorrhages lead to mental disorders. Blockage (embolism) of blood vessels can be considered the cause of this disorder, while embolism can be attributed to a complication of traumatic brain injury, which is accompanied by a fracture of the skull bones.

Mental pathology, which is often observed as a result of a traumatic brain injury, develops through 4 stages:

– elementary;

– spicy;

– convalescence;

– long-term consequences.

The initial period, which occurs immediately after the injury, is usually accompanied by a loss of consciousness, and what will be the level of consciousness in the future, determines the severity and nature of the brain damage. The patient may feel both mildly stunned and in a coma.

The acute period is characterized by the restoration of consciousness, the disappearance of most cerebral disorders. At this time, manifestations of various forms of asthenic syndrome are observed.

If the form of asthenia is defined by physicians as mild, then the following symptoms of nervous disorders are observed: irritability, excessive excitability, headache, sensitivity to light and loud sounds, insomnia. The characteristic features of the acute period include a memory disorder, which is relevant in relation to the very moment of the injury and the sufficiently long period preceding it (from several days to several years).

Also, typical neurological symptoms of the acute period include motor disorders, namely paresis (partial paralysis) and paralysis. Note the presence of hypoesthesia and anesthesia (impaired sensitivity).

If the injury is associated with a fracture of the bones of the base of the skull, then paralysis of the facial nerve occurs. Often the result of traumatic brain injury is intracranial hemorrhage, which leads to compression (compression) of the brain, which can manifest itself in cerebral and local symptoms.

A characteristic sign of the development of the pathology accompanying cranial cerebral trauma is recorded: after the symptoms of the initial period completely disappear and the patient's condition improves, suddenly worsening occurs. Where in there is a sharp headache, which tends to grow rapidly. In patients, the development of signs of lethargy is recorded, and then stoniness is observed.

During a medical examination, a triad of symptoms inherent in the acute period is revealed: arterial and cerebrospinal fluid pressure increase; paresis, paralysis, speech disorders, seizures are fixed; stagnation is observed on the surface of the fundus.

The duration of the patient's stay in the acute period after a cranial cerebral injury of a closed type lasts a minimum of 2 days, a maximum of several months.

Mental disorders accompanying the disease depend entirely on the severity of the injury. They are divided into light, moderate, heavy.

In the first case, patients lose consciousness for a short time, equal to several minutes or even seconds. But the blackout may not happen. In this case, victims may complain of a mild headache, nausea and dizziness.

In the second case, a blackout of consciousness is observed lasting from several minutes to several hours. Then, for another 2 days, a slight stupor is recorded.

Events that preceded trauma and loss of consciousness, as well as those immediately following them.

As a rule, on the first day of the acute period, the patient's consciousness begins to recover, but sometimes this process takes a whole month. At this time, the manifestation of psychoses is recorded, which are characterized by clouding of consciousness, which is attributed to one of 3 types (twilight, delirious and aneroid type).

It should be noted that with delirium, Korsakoff's syndrome sometimes manifests itself, in which memory loss is noted, which has a fixative character (the victims cannot keep current events in memory), retrograde (patients forget the events preceding the loss of consciousness). Somewhat less commonly, anterograde memory loss is observed, in which patients forget the events following the loss of consciousness.

Sometimes mental disorders can manifest themselves in the fact that patients have false memories of events that supposedly happened to them, but did not actually exist. Thus, the consciousness of the victims accepts fictional events as memories. In some cases, patients cannot speak or move (akinetic mutism).

Affective psychoses and hallucinations are less common.

If the patient receives a contusion of the brain, then the acute period may be accompanied by seizures similar to epileptic ones.

If the patient has suffered an injury from a blast wave, then usually a concussion and a bruise of the brain are detected, and hence a violation of cerebral circulation. In this case, the consciousness of a person is suddenly turned off, which can be observed even before the sound of the explosion has reached the auditory receptors.

In this situation, the victim loses consciousness and can be in this state for several minutes or several hours. The sight of him at this moment causes the assumption of a possible death, but after a while he begins to show signs of life. During this period, the victim is indifferent to everything around him, almost does not move and is very lethargic.

The late period in traumatic brain injury is characterized by mental pathologies that can persist without change for at least a year after the injury. However, individual manifestations of these pathologies can undergo a reverse development.

In the post-traumatic period, manifestations are often observed asthenic and psychopathic syndrome, affective and hallucinatory-delusional psychosis. In more severe cases, a state of dementia is recorded.

The most common manifestations of the late period include traumatic asthenia, which is expressed in dizziness, extreme irritability, frequent headaches, and fatigue.

In the warm season, patients feel worse, they do not tolerate transport trips. The impossibility of fast switching associated with various activities is very characteristic.

Sometimes doctors register convulsive seizures in patients during this period, after which a twilight state of consciousness occurs.

With repeated trauma that occurred in the post-traumatic period, or with intoxication, infectious damage to the body, as well as with intense stress, traumatic psychosis may occur. Most likely the appearance of hallucinatory-delusional and affective. In this case, the victim observes a distortion of the perception of reality.

Affective psychoses are characterized by periodic manifestations.

Depression in patients develops in to mania.

In the first case, a melancholy mood is noted, in the second, euphoria is observed, accompanied by a tendency to conflict behavior and explosiveness. Periodically, seizures are recorded, accompanied by clouding of consciousness.

As a rule, affective psychoses do not appear immediately, but appear after 10-20 years. It can be noted that during this period, even a small infection can be a factor provoking acute psychosis.

Hallucinatory-delusional sychoses in victims accompanied by clouding of consciousness, which is referred to as delirium or twilight type.

This disease is characterized by a syndrome of verbal hallucinosis, accompanied by delirium, which is very specific and emotional.

Dementia as a distant consequence of traumatic brain injury is noted relatively rarely. As a rule, it accompanies only severe clinical cases. These include open head injuries and severe concussions of the brain, which are accompanied by fractures of the base of the skull.

Patients in this category are usually lethargic or, on the contrary, excited. The reaction of irritation in them is observed only occasionally in the form of separate outbreaks.

Treatment

The nature of the disease depends on the severity of the injuries. Often, in order to prevent mental pathology threatening after a traumatic brain injury, patients are prescribed bed rest, which they must strictly observe. Along with a complex of therapeutic measures, one should take care of proper nutrition, corresponding to the patient's condition.

The diet of bedridden patients should include a variety of fruits and vegetables in various forms. They are necessary as the main source of vitamins, vegetable fiber and mineral salts. Canned and fresh fruits, kissels, compotes, creams, jellies are shown.

Vitamin therapy plays an important role. Vitamins should enter the patient's body in the form of fruit and berry and vegetable salads, juices, rosehip infusion, yeast drink, wheat bran decoction. Such a diet avoids constipation and has a beneficial effect on the state of the gastrointestinal tract.

It is necessary to reduce the use of flour products (pancakes, pies, white bread). It is recommended to use meat products for food no more than 1 time per day.

You need to eat food in accordance with the regimen 3-4 times a day, slowly, chewing thoroughly. In this case, its calorie content should be no more than 3000 calories.

In the future, as health is restored, the diet should become more high-calorie.

Herbal teas are of great benefit, for which the composition of herbs is selected according to the symptoms. With irritability and nervous excitement, use the foods, infusions and decoctions described above.

With cranial cerebral injuries, the use of alcoholic beverages and beer is absolutely contraindicated.

Traditional medicine recommends the use of teas, infusions and other remedies that are used in the treatment of traumatic brain injury.

Sprouted wheat contains biologically active substances that allow you to activate the process of restoring health, healing wounds. Grapes are also a wound healing agent.

In addition, he is very rich in vitamins.

For headaches, it is recommended to eat pears, raspberries.

Fresh berries, as well as canned sea buckthorn juice, eaten are recommended as a means of enhancing regeneration.

The grenade will have the same effect. In addition, it is a good hematopoietic agent, indicated for blood loss.

Foods rich in vitamin C are necessary for the body in the treatment of traumatic brain injury. A large amount of it contains blackcurrant, rosehip, lemon, orange, cabbage.

To get rid of weakness and

irritability, it is recommended to dilute the juice of 0.5 lemon and 1 tablespoon of honey in 1 glass of hot water. The remedy should be taken in the afternoon, in the evening.

During the recovery period, excellent results in strengthening the nervous system are obtained by using a food product such as bran. They contain a large amount of vitamin B1, which is important for the restoration of nerve cells. They need to be soaked in water, mixed with butter and a little honey and consumed according to the recommendations given on the product packaging.

A decoction of oats with the addition of milk and honey has good sedative (calming) properties. This drink is high in calories.

To prepare a drink, oats are thoroughly washed and poured with water in a ratio of 1: 5, boiled over low heat until the volume is halved.

The resulting jelly is filtered and honey (4 teaspoons) and milk (2 teaspoons) are added to it. Then the mixture is boiled again and drunk in 2-3 doses during the day. If you supplement the treatment with the regular use of a small amount of raisins (it is extremely rich in potassium), then the recovery process is accelerated, overall well-being and mood improve.

Lemon balm tea has excellent taste qualities, it is able to relieve spasms, has an anticonvulsant effect, normalizes the rhythm of heart contractions, has a beneficial effect on the body with neuroses, relieves headaches (like migraine), and alleviates the condition with melancholy.

To make tea, the lemon balm herb is crushed and 2 tablespoons are taken, which are poured with 2 cups of boiling water. When the infusion cools down, it should be strained and drunk during the day, leaving a large portion at night.

Adding sugar is not recommended.

In an asthenic state, the following plants have a stimulating and tonic effect: zamaniha, radiola, Manchurian aralia, leuzea. You should especially dwell on the treatment of post-traumatic asthenia with the help of a lure.

Thanks to the use of alcohol tincture from the rhizome of the lure, you can get rid of neurotic syndromes and asthenic-depressive conditions. Ready tincture is taken before meals 2-3 times a day, 30-40 drops added to boiled water. The course of treatment should not exceed a month.

A noticeable improvement is possible already on the 6-7th day: headaches subside, irritability and fatigue decrease, sleep is normalized.

Psycho endocrine disorders

Psycho endocrine disorders are called mental pathologies that manifest themselves when the humoral regulation of the body deteriorates.

Endocrine diseases are accompanied by the development of mental disorders if there is a direct effect on the body of various pathologies, for example, vascular or hormonal. In addition, the cause of psycho endocrine disorders can be a close relationship between pathology and factors that adversely affect the psyche.

At the initial stage of the development of endocrine pathology, according to M. Bleiler, “endocrine psycho syndromes” appear. They are manifested in a rapid drop in the mental activity of the victim. The expression of the degree of activity, as a rule, is different in each case. The simplest and easiest option is asthenia, accompanied by lethargy and increased fatigue, the most difficult option is a drop in interest in the environment, a decrease in activity to the maximum possible level, as well as a cessation of interaction with the outside world.

The personality of the patient changes greatly, new eating habits, thirst, increased appetite, desire to increase the number of sexual contacts and craving for vagrancy may appear. It is noteworthy that with the development of endocrine pathologies, the habitual inclinations of a person change not qualitatively, but quantitatively. Pathologies in the emotional sphere are manifested by a whole complex, in which there are elements of mania, depression, riddled with outbreaks of unmotivated aggression and malice.

Often there is also joyful excitement in combination with partial motor retardation and physical inactivity.

Frequent attacks of asthenic depression, apathy, unmotivated fear and anxiety.

The patient's mood changes rapidly, affective states are possible, often without obvious reasons. Emotional swings can be both protracted and short-term, occur or intensify only from time to time.

If the endocrine disease is severe and over a long period, a complete mental breakdown is possible. Memory and mental abilities are rapidly deteriorating, emotional activity decreases, the likelihood of developing dementia increases.

With Sheehen's disease and Simmonds' pituitary cachexia, pituitary insufficiency is observed, which is accompanied by weakness and fatigue. The movements of patients are slow, so they give the impression of being imbecile, although in reality they are not. A serious decrease in intelligence is possible only in the later stages of the development of the disease.

Addison's disease is accompanied by mental and physical weakness of the affected person. The patient often demonstrates flashes of uncontrollable emotional upsurge and gets tired just as quickly.

The development of acromegaly is accompanied by symptoms such as lethargy, apathy, replaced by euphoria. The patient is absolutely passive and does not show interest in the environment, being content only with himself. A decrease in intellectual abilities is rarely manifested; in the worst case, a person begins to narrow his circle of interests.

With hyperthyroidism, the patient has sleep disturbances, which is accompanied by disturbing dreams and frequent awakenings. Brain activity is practically not affected. The patient's movements become fussy, and the reaction is quick, but he is not able to concentrate his attention on one thing.

With hypothyroidism, mental pathology is much more significant. Often with this disease, the presence of congenital dementia is noted. The mood of the patient, as a rule, is good, but sometimes there are outbursts of irritation, accompanied by displeased mumbling.

The female psyche and an excess or lack of sex hormones are closely related, that is, the psyche can affect the menstrual cycles and vice versa. Often in mental illnesses such as epilepsy and schizophrenia, menstruation is very irregular and painful. If a girl has a genetic predisposition to mental illness, especially schizophrenia, her first menstruation begins between the ages of 15 and 17.

With the development of manic-depressive psychosis, menstruation may stop, and begin again only after the onset of recovery. Experts are sure that the only accurate indicator of a woman's mental state is her menstrual cycle, of course, if the violations of this cycle are not associated with diseases that carry gynecological character.

If a woman has a mental illness that has not previously manifested itself in any way, was latent, then during the menstrual cycle it may worsen.

Approximately 70% of women suffer from symptoms of premenstrual syndrome, manifested as a complex of mental, somatic and endocrine pathologies. Symptoms appear 2-4 days before the onset of menstruation and partially disappear after they begin.

Premenstrual syndrome is based on disorders psyche, which are accompanied by various pathologies. As a rule, in adolescence and adulthood, the symptoms of premenstrual syndrome are mild, but as they grow older, they become more pronounced.

Just before the onset of menstruation, a woman's behavior

changes dramatically. Her calm and balanced character can instantly change to the exact opposite.

Outbursts of rage, whims and unmotivated irritation by others accompany the entire premenstrual period. The woman becomes aggressive and suspicious.

If the listed symptoms do not disappear with the onset of menstruation, it is necessary to be examined by a psychiatrist and gynecologist, since these symptoms may signal the development of a disease.

If a woman suffers from any diseases of the internal organs, during menstruation they can become aggravated, as the body is subjected to severe overload and is not able to provide sufficient resistance to the disease.

Treatment

For the treatment of endocrine psychoses, most of the efforts should be directed to increasing immunity and restoring the body's strength. For this, special vitamin teas are best suited, which in a relatively short time can give the patient new strength.

Vitamin tea number 1

Collect fresh rose hips and black currants in a ratio of 1: 1, chop, put in a glass container, pour 0.5 liters of boiling water and close the lid tightly. Infuse for 1-2 hours. Strain and add sugar to taste. Take orally daily 2-3 times a day for 0.5-1 glass.

Vitamin tea number 2

200 g rose hips, 200 g lingonberries and a few leaves nettles carefully chop and pour 1 liter of boiling water. Put on low heat, boil for 5-10 minutes, and then insist for 5 hours in a dark place under a tightly closed lid. Strain the finished tea, add sugar to taste and take chilled

daily, 0.3 cups 2-3 times a day after meals.

Anorexia nervosa

This disease is a pathological mental disorder that usually occurs in adolescence, when a sick teenager refuses to eat in order to noticeably lose weight.

The causes of the onset and development of anorexia nervosa are not fully understood by science. But among experts there is an opinion that the cause of this mental disorder can be both biological and psychological characteristics of a sick child. Often, anorexia nervosa syndrome develops against the background of neuroses, psychopathy, and even some endocrine disorders. In addition, experts believe that such a pathology occurs in those families where one of the relatives suffered from mental illness, character anomalies or alcoholism.

With the development of this disease, the importance of education is also important, for example, in hyper-custody (when parents pay excessive attention to their children) or in a family where conflict situations often develop. In such cases, the child has a special reaction to any actions of the parents. And the impetus for the development of the disease is a disharmonic teenage crisis.

Most often, girls aged 14–18 suffer from anorexia nervosa syndrome. But in recent years, the incidence rate has increased to such an extent that the medical term "anorexic explosion in the population" has arisen. There are even cases when men are also affected by this disease.

Patients with anorexia nervosa have specific character traits. So, for example, such patients are characterized by: punctuality (to the point of pedantry), pride, manic determination, accuracy in everything, a tendency to overvalued ideas, and pathological attachment to the mother (mainly in childhood).

Usually, the impetus for the development of the disease is the words of those around the teenager that he is disfigured by fullness. After such words, the teenager convinces himself that he is ugly, and finds a way out in starvation. Thus, anorexia nervosa is closely related to adolescent dysmorphia.

Pathology begins with the fact that a teenager gradually limits himself in certain foods that, in his opinion, are too high in calories. As the disease progresses, the teenager continues to deprive himself of more and more food by willpower. At the same time, he constantly feels a feeling of hunger, but does not satisfy the need organism. At first, the inner struggle of a sick child is not seen by others, but over time, his behavior changes so much that parents notice the oddities in their child's behavior.

They try to get him to eat, but the teen shows unusual ingenuity, such as hiding the food or throwing it away. If you still have to eat, then he artificially induces vomiting or takes laxatives.

At the initial stage of the disease, patients exhaust themselves with heavy physical exertion, while avoiding physical tranquility by any means, preferring to do everything on the go.

Over time, the patient has not only external changes, but also mental ones. At the same time, he becomes anxious, suspicious, irritable, after which he develops depression. In severe cases, patients look emaciated, lethargic, move less and less. At the same time, the circle of their interests is gradually narrowing.

Due to exhaustion in patients with anorexia nervosa, endocrine disorders begin. In this case, a noticeable decrease in body weight from 10 to 50 percent of the initial body weight is possible. The skin becomes pale, dry, flaky, acquires an earthy hue. The patient's extremities are cold to the touch. In addition to endocrine disorders, vitamin deficiency is observed.

Due to constant starvation, patients suffer from constipation, and after eating they complain of spastic pains in the abdomen.

In addition, in girls with anorexia nervosa, increased body hair growth and amenorrhea (cessation of menstrual cycles) begins. Restoration of the cycle occurs only with the normalization of nutrition, when body weight reaches 48–50 kg.

Anorexia nervosa is characterized by an undulating course, with relapses occurring throughout adolescence. Girls are easier to treat than male patients.

It should be noted that refusal to

eat is characteristic not only for anorexia nervosa, but also for depression.

Treatment

In the treatment of anorexia nervosa, patients with harmful cases are admitted to the hospital. Typically, these patients are treated on an outpatient basis.

The main goal of the treatment of patients with anorexia nervosa is the restoration of body weight, as well as the restoration of all systems in which pathological disorders are observed.

In addition, the doctor conducts tests to determine the level of sugar in blood, after which he prescribes a course of vitamin therapy and restorative agents. If necessary, blood substitutes are also used.

The most important thing in the treatment of patients with anorexia nervosa is the establishment of a proper diet. At the initial stages, food intake occurs in small doses (6-7 times a day). At the same time, it should be high-calorie and at the same time light, not coarse.

If the doctor sees that the patient is noticeably gaining weight (from 2-3 kg or more), then the therapy is proceeding successfully.

A patient with anorexia nervosa should eat foods with a high content of proteins, fats and vitamins.

The composition of this diet should include a sufficient amount of fresh fruits, vegetables, berries, leafy greens, nuts, as well as milk, kefir, cheese, eggs, cottage cheese, meat, offal, fish, smoked meats. These are the foods that contain the right amount of nutrients. At the same time, one should not forget that a large amount of fats and carbohydrates should not be included in the diet of a patient with anorexia nervosa.

The patient's diet should contain the required amount of vitamins in the form of raw vegetable and fruit juices, as well as decoctions of wild rose, black currant, yeast drink. To quickly restore the strength of the patient's body, it is necessary to add to the diet include mineral salts, especially calcium salts, which are found in dairy products, eggshells, and leafy greens.

Thus, the most important thing during the treatment of patients with anorexia nervosa is to determine the dose of certain products, which include a sufficient amount of proteins, vitamins and fats.

Presenile (presenile) psychoses

A number of mental disorders can sometimes be observed at the age of reverse development. The endocrine system undergoes significant changes during this period, which can occur with violations of its functions. An important role in the occurrence of presenile psychoses is played by the presence of somatic (diseases of sensory and nerve fibers) and psychogenic diseases (diseases that occur as a reaction to mental trauma), which can be provoking factors.

These diseases include depression, involution melancholia) and delusional psychosis (involution paranoid).

With involution paranoid, the so-called delirium of ordinary relations is observed, which is combined with delirium of damage. Patients become suspicious, anxiety affects their behavior. For example, it begins to seem to them that neighbors come into their apartment and take things that belong to them, patients believe that their acquaintances spoil their food or things.

People suffering from involution paranoia accuse their relatives of not taking measures to prevent intruders, trying to turn to the police for help.

When defending their interests, patients are energetic, active, proving their case with the help of a mass of arguments. They are trying to attract witnesses to this process. Since delirium is of a mundane nature, and there is a sequence in the presentation of complaints, relatives and friends may not immediately see signs of an incipient disease in such behavior.

Sometimes relatives of patients observe not only the delirium of ordinary relationships, but also other types of delirium. Those suffering from involution paranoia express their belief that unknown individuals are trying to poison them by adding harmful substances to their food. This delusional assumption makes patients strictly control the process of cooking, in some cases refuse to eat. In this case, we can talk about the delirium of poisoning. The delirium of jealousy can also join the listed manifestations.

At the same time, the presence of uncritical attitude towards oneself, a monotonously elevated mood, excessive thoroughness as a form of violation of thinking.

Evolutionary melancholy begins after a short stages of harbingers in the form of various ailments,

AIDS. Sometimes patients are sure that there is they have a similar disease.

Evolutional melancholia is characterized by both vegetative symptoms (tachycardia, dyspepsia, sweating) and sense to pithy (moving nerves and blood vessels, crawling, etc.). Patients behave not properly. They repeatedly visit doctors, insisting on numerous tests, examinations of their body. At the same time, they strictly follow a diet and regimen that they themselves consider useful.

During the acute period, patients are in a serious condition, close to despair. They rush about in anticipation of terrible events (the death of loved ones, execution or any kind of torment). Such agitated depression is accompanied by a distortion of the perception of reality, which becomes illusory.

In the behavior of others, in their conversations, in the whole environment, patients hear and see accusations, threats and condemnations against them, often they refuse food. During this period, those suffering from involution melancholy should be hospitalized and be under strict medical supervision.

During the illness, which is very long, such patients quickly lose weight, they show premature decrepitude. However, the patient's condition gradually stabilizes. Various disorders lose their vividness, and depressive delirium stops. The sick are recovering.

Treatment

People suffering from presenile psychoses need vigorous restorative therapy. Vitamin therapy should play an important role in it. Patients especially need B vitamins, namely B1 and B6. Vitamin C should play a positive role in alleviating the patient's condition. Proper rational and nutritious nutrition should be attributed to important factors in the prevention of the above diseases and premature aging. If, starting from the age of 45, efforts are not made to correct nutritional deficiencies, then the likelihood of metabolic disorders increases greatly, which creates prerequisites for the possible emergence and development of presenile psychoses.

Often occurring in old age with malnutrition, fullness in itself contributes to the development of atherosclerosis, hypertension, diabetes mellitus, etc. In this case, some food restrictions are necessary, and a diet should be followed.

A dairy-vegetarian diet has a

beneficial effect on the body. With presenile psychosis, the patient's diet should include various fruits and vegetables as a source of vitamins, vegetable fiber and essential mineral salts.

Here is a list of recommended dishes: vegetable, fruit, milk soups, soups cooked in weak fish and meat broths. Recommended fish dishes (from sea fish), cottage cheese. Fruits, fresh, dried and canned, as well as in the form of compotes and jelly are especially useful. Yeast drink, rosehip infusion is shown.

Meat should be eaten no more than once a day, and it is necessary to limit its consumption to dishes with boiled or steamed meat.

Fatty meats, ham, smoked sausages and other smoked meats, sweet confectionery products (cakes, sweets, buns, etc.), flour products (pies, pancakes) should not be eaten (or reduced to a minimum).

It is recommended to use rye or wheat bread baked from whole meal flour.

Food should consist of dishes that are not high in calories. It is necessary to establish a mode of eating, switching to 4 meals a day strictly at a certain time. Patients should chew food well, so you should always maintain the oral cavity, teeth in good condition.

Application Diets

In the treatment of diseases of the nervous system, special diets are used, the purpose of which is to restore the body's strength after an illness. They are based on determining the body's individual need for nutrients and energy, taking into account the nature of metabolic disorders, the stage of the disease, age and anthropometric indicators, as well as the optimal use in the diet of such biologically active substances as vitamins, minerals, lipotropic factors, antioxidants, each of which plays a specific role.

When drawing up a specific diet, it is necessary to take into account the individual characteristics of each patient. So, in some diseases, adherence to a certain diet is the main therapeutic measure, in others it serves as a background, without which the main therapy will be ineffective.

In diseases prone to a long, recurrent course, it is recommended to adhere to an appropriate diet for a long time. If the patient's condition improves, sparing diets are gradually replaced by more physically complete ones, which, in terms of food composition and energy value, are close to the diet of a healthy person.

Physiologically complete diets are prescribed for a long-term, and defective - for a short time, which is determined by the doctor, taking into account the severity of the course of the disease.

Diet #1

Indicated in anorexia nervosa. Assign in the first days of treatment, no longer than 2 weeks. The goal of the diet is to reduce inflammation and improve defect healing by limiting thermal, mechanical, and chemical stimuli.

Calorie content is 1800-1900 kcal. Calorie reduction is achieved primarily by restricting carbohydrate intake. The temperature of hot dishes should be no higher than 50-55 ° C, cold dishes - no lower than 15-20 ° C.

From the diet should be excluded substances that increase gastric secretion, as well as mechanical, chemical and thermal stimuli. Sour-milk drinks, cheese, sour cream, ordinary cottage cheese are contraindicated. Food prepared in liquid or mushy form should be taken in small portions at least 6 times a day.

The following dishes and products are recommended:

– mucous soups from semolina, oatmeal, rice, pearl barley with the addition of an egg-milk mixture, butter or cream;

– lean fish dishes cooked for a couple;

– dairy products (milk, cream, steamed soufflé from mashed cottage cheese);

– soft-boiled eggs or steam omelet;

– liquid cereal milk porridge;

– cereals made from buckwheat or oatmeal with the addition of cream or milk;

– jelly and jelly made from sweet fruits or berries, sugar,

honey;

– fresh butter and vegetable oil, which is added to

dishes;

– Weak tea with milk or cream, juices from fresh berries and fruits diluted with water.

– Diet #2

The diet is used for the same disease as diet No. 1, however, it is prescribed at subsequent stages of treatment while maintaining bed rest for the patient. The duration of diet therapy is 10-14 days. The intended purpose is the same as that of diet No. 1.

Food is boiled or steamed, consumed in a semi-liquid or puree form. Milk and dairy products are widely used. Fried foods are excluded. Calorie content 2300–2400 kcal. The total amount of free fluid is 2 liters. The temperature of hot dishes should be no higher than 55-60 ° C, and cold - no lower than 15-20

°C.

Instead of bread, it is allowed to consume from 75 to 100 g per day of dried (not fried) crackers. All products and dishes from meat and fish listed in diet No. 1 are prepared in the form of a steam soufflé, mashed potatoes, and cutlets. The rest of the recommendations are similar to diet number 1.

Diet number 3 basic)

It is universal in the treatment of diseases of the nervous system. The purpose of the diet is the same as for diet No. 1, but it is less sparing than diet No. 2.

Food should be liquid, mushy (more dense consistency of products is also allowed), boiled or mashed. Limit the use of foods high in fiber. Calorie content 2800-2900 kcal. The total amount of free fluid is 1.5 liters. Food temperature is normal.

Rye and any fresh bread, pastry and puff pastry products, meat and fish broths, mushroom and strong vegetable broths, borscht, cabbage soup, okroshka, fatty and stringy meats and poultry, duck, goose, smoked meats, canned meat, dairy products with high acidity, millet, barley and barley groats, legumes, pasta, white cabbage, swede, turnip, radish, onion, sorrel, salted, pickled and pickled vegetables.

The following dishes and products are recommended:

– dried wheat bread from premium flour;

– soups from mashed and well-boiled cereals cooked in vegetable broth, milk soups seasoned with butter, egg-and-milk mixture or cream, vegetable puree soups;

– steam and boiled dishes of beef, young low-fat lamb, trimmed pork, turkey and chickens;

– boiled or steamed lean fish without skin, fish cakes;

– milk, cream, non-sour curdled milk and kefir, curd soufflé or pudding, lazy dumplings;

– semi-viscous, mashed semolina, buckwheat, rice porridge, boiled in water or milk;

– potatoes, carrots, beets, cauliflower, boiled or steamed, as well as soufflés, mashed potatoes or steamed puddings thereof;

– boiled vegetable salad, boiled tongue, boiled sausage without fat;

– jellied fish on a vegetable decoction;

– fruit purees, jelly, jelly, pureed compotes, sugar, honey;

– weak tea with the addition of milk or cream, sweet fruit and berry juices;

– Butter and refined sunflower oil added to dishes.

Here it is necessary to take into account the stage of the disease, as well as the severity of its clinical manifestations. So, for example, with the attenuation of acute phenomena, the patient is transferred to diet No. 1.

Diet number 4

It is recommended for stress and hangover in order to restore the functioning of the gastrointestinal tract.

Diet number 4 refers to physically complete diets with the restriction of the use of foods containing coarse fiber, as well as whole milk, spicy foods, snacks and spices. Food should be well chopped. Fried foods are allowed, but without a rough crust, so you should fry without breading. Calorie 2800 kcal.The total amount of liquid is 1.5 liters. Food temperature is normal.

The following foods and dishes are recommended:

– yesterday's wheat bread;

– soups cooked in weak meat or fish broth, vegetable broth with finely chopped and well-boiled vegetables or grated cereals;

– boiled, baked, fried without a rough crust low-fat meat and poultry, meatballs;

– boiled or baked lean fish;

– kefir, curdled milk, fresh cottage cheese, added in dishes and drinks milk and cream;

– snacks and salads from fresh tomatoes, boiled vegetables with meat, fish and eggs;

– Mashed ripe fruits and berries, baked apples.

– Diet number 5

It is indicated for atherosclerosis of cerebral vessels.

The diet contains physiological the norm of proteins, fats and carbohydrates, as well as vitamins and minerals. It includes dishes rich in vegetable fiber, which should not irritate the mucous membrane of the gastrointestinal tract. Calorie content 2500-2900 kcal.

Foods rich in essential oils, cholesterol, fat breakdown products formed during the frying process are excluded from the diet. Spicy and fatty sauces, horseradish, pepper, mustard are contraindicated. Vegetables and fruits are consumed raw, boiled and baked. Food is not crushed, steamed or boiled.

The following dishes and products are recommended:

– rye or wheat bread from whole meal flour, bran or grain, yesterday's baking;

– soups cooked in weak fat-free meat or fish broth, vegetable broth, mainly vegetable with pearl barley;

– boiled or baked piece of lean meat, poultry, fish;

– crumbly cereals and casseroles from buckwheat, millet, wheat, barley groats;

– raw or boiled vegetables for garnish (beets, carrots, tomatoes, lettuce, cucumbers, zucchini, pumpkin) and casseroles from them;

– fresh vegetable salads, vinaigrettes seasoned with vegetable oil;

– fresh ripe sweet fruits and berries raw or in dishes, soaked dried apricots or prunes;

– tea and coffee drinks (from substitutes);

– Sauces on weak meat, fish broth, milk sauce.

– Diet number 6

It is used in the same way as the previous diet for atherosclerosis of cerebral vessels. The duration of diet therapy is 5-8 days.

Caloric content is reduced to 2000 kcal by limiting the intake of carbohydrates and fats. The content of proteins corresponds to the physiological norm. Foods containing coarse fiber, fresh bread, rich bakery products, spices, pickles, coffee, cocoa, cold and carbonated drinks, whole milk and other dairy products, snacks are excluded from the diet. The total amount of liquid is 1.5 liters.

The following dishes and products are recommended:

- about 200 g of wheat bread crackers from premium flour;

- soups prepared on fat-free low meat or fish broth with the addition of mucous decoctions of pearl barley, semolina or rice groats, boiled mashed meat, steam dumplings, meatballs, egg flakes;

- boiled cutlets, dumplings or meatballs from lean and non-fat beef, veal or turkey, boiled meat soufflé;

- lean fish, boiled or steamed in the form of cutlets, meatballs or a piece;

- freshly prepared calcined or mashed unleavened cottage cheese;

- 1-2 soft-boiled eggs or steam omelet;

- mashed rice, oatmeal, buckwheat porridge, boiled in water;

– vegetables only in the form of decoctions, which added to soups;

– Green tea, black coffee and milk-free cocoa, diluted fruit juices, with the exception of grape, plum and apricot.

– Diet number 7

Indicated for migraine. Depending on the nature of the course of the disease, the duration of diet therapy is from 2 to 4 weeks. Diet refers to physically complete. Content it contains proteins, fats and carbohydrates corresponds to the physiological norm. The consumption of table salt, mechanical and chemical irritants of the mucous membrane and the receptor apparatus of the gastrointestinal tract is moderately limited. Excluded are products that enhance fermentation processes, and stimulants of gastric secretion and bile secretion. Calorie content 2700-2900 kcal.

Products are boiled or steamed,

wiped. Soups should also be pureed or contain finely chopped vegetables and well-boiled cereals, baked dishes are allowed, without a rough crust.

The following dishes and products are recommended:

– wheat bread from flour of the highest or first grade, dried or yesterday's baking;

– soups cooked in weak meat, fish broth or vegetable broth with meatballs, dumplings;

– minced meat, chicken, turkey, boiled or steamed;

– lean fish, in pieces, minced, boiled or steamed;

– milk, cream, sour cream added to dishes, kefir, acidophilus, curdled milk, freshly prepared cottage cheese;

– 1-2 soft-boiled eggs or scrambled eggs;

– well-boiled cereals from various cereals in water or with the addition of milk;

– boiled and pureed vegetables (potatoes, carrots, cauliflower);

– ripe and sweet fruits and berries without peel;

– sauces on weak meat, fish broths, as well as dairy.

– Diet number 8

It is used for hypertension.

The diet limits the amount of fat and salt. It excludes food substances containing purines, cholesterol, coarse fiber, fried foods, black bread, fatty meat and fish, internal organs of animals, meat, fish and mushroom broths, raw vegetables and fruits, garlic, onions and spices. Calorie content 2350–2700 kcal. Food is taken 5-6 times a day.

The following dishes and products are recommended:

– wheat bread from flour of the highest and first grade, dried or yesterday's baking;

– vegetarian soups with mashed vegetables, puree soups, creams, milk soups mixed with water;

– lean beef, chicken, turkey, rabbit, boiled

– low-fat boiled fish, fish cakes;

– steam and baked protein omelets;

– mashed rice and semolina porridge, boiled in milk in half with water, as well as porridge from buckwheat or flour;

– boiled and mashedvegetables;

– ripe, soft, sweet fruits and berries, raw or rubbed;

– Tea with lemon, milk, sweet fruit and berry juices.

– Diet number 9 (sparing)

Used for anorexia nervosa. This is a diet with a normal content of easily digestible proteins, a significant restriction of fats and easily absorbed carbohydrates. The amount of table salt should not exceed 6 g per day. All dishes should be boiled or mashed steam. Fried foods are excluded, and sweets are sharply limited. Fatty meat and fish, vegetable oil, raw vegetables and fruits, radishes, radishes, onions, garlic, meat, fish and mushroom broths are prohibited. Calorie content 2000–2200 kcal.

The following dishes and products are recommended:

– wheat bread from yesterday's baking, wheat bread crackers;

– mashed vegetable soups,

cereals cooked in vegetable broth, carrot or cauliflower puree soups;

– lean meat and fish in the form of soufflés, dumplings, steam cutlets, boiled chicken in pieces;

– 1 egg per day in the form of a protein steam omelet or protein soufflé;

– milk, provided it is well tolerated, unleavened low-fat cottage cheese in the form of soufflé, puddings, sour cream only as a condiment;

– not sharpcheese;

– boiled, stewed or baked vegetables (potatoes, pumpkin, cauliflower, zucchini, carrots);

– pureed compotes, kissels, mousses and jelly from ripe sweet fruits and berries;

– milk and sour cream sauces, fruit sauces;

– fruit, berry juicesand decoctions.

www.ingramcontent.com/pod-product-compliance
Lightning Source LLC
LaVergne TN
LVHW012040160826
845678LV00014B/2649